BEAT THE CRAPS TABLE

BEAT THE
CRAPS
TABLE

MARTEN JENSEN

CARDOZA PUBLISHING

Copyright © 2003 by Marten Jensen
-All Rights Reserved-

First Edition

Library of Congress Catalog Card No.: 2003100558
ISBN: 1-58042-093-1

Visit our web site (www.cardozapub.com) or write us for a full list of Cardoza books, advanced, and computer strategies.

CARDOZA PUBLISHING
1-800-577-WINS
P.O. Box 1500, Cooper Station, New York, NY 10276

TABLE OF CONTENTS

1. INTRODUCTION   **9**
It's All Here   12
Acknowledgements   12
A Note on Personal Pronouns   12

2. CRAPS FUNDAMENTALS   **13**
The Equipment   13
The Personnel   17
Object of the Game   19
The Shooter   21
The Come-out Roll   22
The Point Phase   23

3. PLAYING IN THE CASINO   **25**
Selecting a Table   25
Obtaining Chips and Credit   26
The Wagers   27
Placing Bets   30
Rolling the Dice   32
Table Etiquette   34
Tipping   36

4. UNDERSTANDING THE ODDS   **38**
The Dice Combinations   38
The Meaning of Odds   40

5. THE PASS LINE AND COME WAGERS   **44**
The Pass Line Wager   44
The Come Wager   46
Taking Odds   49

6. THE DON'T PASS AND DON'T COME WAGERS   54

Right and Wrong Bettors   54
The Don't Pass Wager   55
The Don't Come Wager   57
Laying Odds   58
Special Note on the House Edge   61

7. THE PLACE NUMBER WAGERS   64

The Place Bet   64
The Buy Bet   67
The Lay Bet   68

8. THE REMAINING BETS   70

The Field Bet   70
The Big 6 and Big 8 Bets   71
The Proposition Bets   73
One-Roll Wagers   75

9. SUMMARY OF ALL CRAPS WAGERS   78

Chart of Line Wagers   78
Chart of Multi-Roll Wagers   79
Chart of One-Roll Wagers   80

10. MONEY MANAGEMENT   81

Controlling Your Bankroll   81
Personal Betting Limits   83
When to Quit   84
Money Management Reminders   85
Dealing with the IRS   86

11. THE FUNDAMENTALS OF CRAPS
BETTING STRATEGY   89

General Betting Advice   89
Qualifying the Shooter   90
An Elementary Strategy   92
Example of Elementary Strategy   93
Common Strategy Errors   94

12. BETTING WITH THE DICE   **97**
     Conservative Strategy   97
     Example of Conservative Strategy   99
     Conventional Strategy   101
     Example of Conventional Strategy   103
     Aggressive Strategy   105

13. BETTING AGAINST THE DICE   **108**
     Conservative Don't Strategy   109
     Example of Conservative Don't Strategy   112
     Conventional Don't Strategy   113
     Aggressive Don't Strategy   114

14. DICE CONTROL   **116**
     Setting the Dice   118
     Gripping the Dice   120
     Throwing the Dice   120
     Spotting a Control Shooter   121

15. OTHER CRAPS GAMES   **123**
     Crapless Craps   123
     Private Craps Games   125

APPENDIX   **128**
     House Edge Calculations   128
     Pass-Line Bet   129
     Don't Pass Bet   130
     Don't Pass Bet with Odds   131

GLOSSARY   **132**

1

INTRODUCTION

Between the covers of *Beat the Craps Table*, you will find everything you need to know about craps, and a lot more. The game is described in full detail and includes all the information on odds and payoffs that you will ever need. A variety of playing strategies are fully described, and these are the tried and true strategies used for years and years by the most accomplished craps players. In the following pages, you will not find any novel or oddball strategies; nor will you find strategies that are not mathematically sound and have no history of successes.

This book is as suitable and useful for the beginning player as it is for the experienced player. It contains a full chapter on money management, including a section on how to deal with the IRS. The chapter on playing in the casino includes advice on how to select a table, how to properly make wagers, as well as a little about the culture of the game, including tipping protocol. For the more advanced player, there is a chapter on dice control.

This book has another feature not found in most other craps books. There is no chitchat, not a single personal anecdote, and no gambling stories. It is packed solid with useful data, facts, and the very best playing information. You will find none of the extraneous and non-informative material that is often used to fill out a gambling book.

Of the many kinds of games available in casinos, craps is, without a doubt, the fastest and most exciting of them all.

BEAT THE CRAPS TABLE

The game is favored by players who want action and the opportunity to make a variety of wagers whenever they want to. Not only that, but when the odds bet is utilized, the house advantage for the best wagers on the table is the lowest to be found anywhere—less than ½ of one percent.

So, how can the casino earn money on a game with such a low house edge? Most players don't know to take advantage of the odds offered by the casino; they tend to make sucker bets on which the house earns a high percentage. They do this because they haven't studied the game and don't know which are the best bets and which are the worst. Furthermore, many people use a willy-nilly betting approach and don't have a rational, thought-out playing strategy. This is because they never learned how to play the game properly, and many casinos seem to like it that way.

The main problem with craps is that the action tends to overwhelm a new player, and most casinos don't address this issue. They act as though the supply of new craps players is infinite. My brother-in-law, who has been dealing craps in Nevada for twenty-seven years, wrote a monograph in which he describes a new player's first impressions in the following way:

> A new player walking up to a busy craps table will at first feel like he's stumbled upon some arcane tribal ritual with people saying and doing things that he cannot comprehend. If there are reasons for this behavior, they are beyond his understanding. Sixteen people will be shouting at the top of their lungs; some of them will just be cheering, others will be issuing instructions to the dealers in some indecipherable code that the dealers appear to actually understand, for some inexplicable reason. Chips will be moving around like pieces on a board game, sometimes they will move to a spot on the table where they will sit for an indeterminate period of time and eventually disappear.

INTRODUCTION

Occasionally the dealer will pay a bet, point to a player and say, "This is yours." How does he know?

The stickman, who seems to be directing the game, will be chanting some codified mantra which makes no sense at all to the new player, but which others seem to either understand or ignore altogether: "Sir, your Hard Eight fell...Would you like that World Bet? ... Place the Inside Numbers...I've got your Hardways working...Hop the 4/10 Hard three from the pole, Two-Way Yo on the outside corner, thank you, sir" etc. Is this gibberish or... well, or what?

The other two dealers are equally wrapped up in the ritual, speaking in tongues, as is the stickman, but ranting in a different language. "No, sir, you were Off on the Come-Out roll...Press it one unit...Down with Twenty-five...That's Eighty-Five Inside out of one hundred...No action on the paper...Marker Up, One-Thousand, my first."

It's chaos, but it's controlled chaos.

I couldn't have said it better myself—controlled chaos! This book will overcome all of that and teach you how to play the game to give you the best chance of winning. It will teach you about all the bets available on the craps table, the correct (actual) odds for every bet, and the house payoff odds. It will train you to detect the most favorable bets and to know which ones to avoid. It will also teach you how to calculate the odds yourself as well as how to play the game properly, using the best playing strategies, from the most conservative to the most aggressive. You will learn how to control your bankroll and your playing session stake, when to quit playing and when it is not yet time to quit. Everything there is to know about the game of casino craps is at your fingertips, and when you are done, the game will no longer be *controlled chaos*.

IT'S ALL HERE

The bookstores carry many books on how to play craps. So what does this book offer that the others don't? Craps books fall into a number of categories, most of which are unsuitable for the average recreational craps player. They may oversimplify the game for rank beginners and provide no information beyond the basic rudiments of craps. Alternatively, they may be directed at the expert player and contain hardly any of the basics. Some books come up with strange, far-out betting strategies that are guaranteed to win the money. Other books offer time worn betting systems that are guaranteed to keep you from losing. You may have already wasted your money on one or more of these books, and found out that it didn't help you very much.

ACKNOWLEDGMENTS

My special thanks to Michael Shackleford (The Wizard of Odds) for checking and verifying my math. I would also like to thank my brother-in-law and master craps dealer, Ben Dicksion, for providing me with valuable insight on the game of craps, as well as for the extract from his monograph in this Introduction. And, of course, I would like to thank my dear wife DeAnna, whose astute suggestions and skillful manuscript editing helped make this a better book.

A NOTE ON PERSONAL PRONOUNS

To avoid the awkward "he or she" or "his/her" grammatical constructions, this book uses the convention of applying masculine pronouns to players and dealers. This was an arbitrary choice for convenience of writing and does not carry any implications. Obviously, all dealers and players are not men.

2

CRAPS FUNDAMENTALS

If you expect to win at casino craps, it goes without saying that you need to know and understand the odds, the payoffs, and the best wagers in as much depth as possible. Before jumping over to the strategy chapters, it would be time well spent to first read and absorb these early chapters, especially if you are a beginner or novice. If you are a more experienced player, at least review the material because I guarantee you will learn *something*.

THE EQUIPMENT

The Craps Table
Unlike other table games, craps tables vary considerably in size. The typical craps table accommodates sixteen to twenty standing players, and is manned by a crew of four: a stickman, two inside dealers, and a boxman. The largest tables, which can handle up to twenty-four standing players, often have two boxmen. Occasionally, you may find a very small table that is run by a single dealer and accommodates eight or nine seated players.

Regardless of size, all craps tables have high sides to contain the action of the dice. At both ends, the inside surfaces of the sides are covered with diamond-embossed rubber. This is where the thrown dice are supposed to bounce to assure a fair roll. The central portion of the long side opposite the boxman is mirrored so that he can easily see the opposite faces of the dice to ascertain that someone didn't switch in misspotted cubes.

The tops of the sides have rails with convenient grooves that hold the player's chips. Lower down on the outside is a ledge for holding drinks and ashtrays.

The felt surface of the craps table carries the imprinted betting layout, which has numerous boxes and spaces for placing wagers. To a newcomer, the layout may seem very complex, but as the nature and purpose of the various bets are explained it will eventually become clear and logical. A typical double-ended craps layout is shown on the next page.

Almost all craps tables are double-ended, meaning that the layout is duplicated at both ends of the table to make the betting areas easier to reach by all the players. These end sections contain the most important and useful bets on the table. Between the two end sections is a large box containing the center bets, also known as the proposition bets, all of which are controlled by the stickman. The wagers shown on the layout, along with some other bets that are not shown, will be explained fully in the following chapters.

The Dice
Modern casino dice are precision-made cubes of cellulose acetate. The faces are micro-lapped to an accuracy of $1/10,000^{th}$ of an inch so that they are perfectly square, flat, and parallel, making each of the dice as precisely cubical as possible. Most dice have flush number spots, and to maintain the correct weight and balance, each spot is slightly recessed and filled with a colored paint that is the same weight as the material that was removed. Casino dice have sharp edges rather than the rounded edges found on backgammon or home-game dice.

CRAPS FUNDAMENTALS

THE LAYOUT OF A CRAPS TABLE

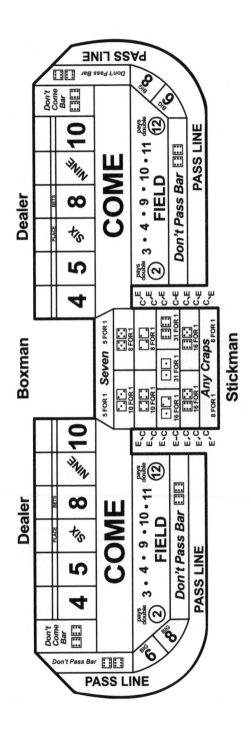

BEAT THE CRAPS TABLE

Standard casino dice in most of the world are 0.750-inch wide, but a few casinos may use slightly smaller dice. Each cube is usually embossed with the casino logo and a code number to make it difficult for cheats to switch in dishonest dice.

Each of the dice has six faces, with each of the faces having one through six spots. The game of craps uses a pair of dice, so that the possible numbers that can be rolled are 2 through 12. A thorough discussion of the various dice combinations, as well as the odds and probabilities in craps are covered in a later chapter.

The Puck

A round plastic disk, black on one side and white on the other, is used to indicate when a point is established. This disk is called a **puck**, although in the past it has sometimes been called a buck. During a come-out roll the black side of the puck, which is marked with the word OFF, is lying face up. When a point number is rolled, the puck is turned over and placed at the appropriate numbered box to remind everyone which point was established. The white side of the puck (marked ON) is now facing up. The puck remains in this position until the point is made or the shooter sevens-out, whereupon it is removed from the number box and flipped to its black side.

THE TWO SIDES OF A PUCK

The Chips

The game of craps is played with casino chips. As with most table games, you can throw a bill on the table and say, "Cash plays," but you will be paid off with casino chips. The preferred and most widely accepted procedure is to drop some currency in front of the nearest dealer and ask for chips. The dealer will ask what denomination you want and then will place a stack in front of you.

In most casinos, $1 chips are white, $5 chips are red (called nickels or reds), $25 chips are green (called quarters or greens), and $100 chips are black. In the few casinos that modify this color scheme, the differences will quickly become apparent. The minimum denomination used in most casinos is $1, but you may encounter 25-cent chips in very low-limit games.

The term **cheque** (pronounced *check*) is used by casino personnel, high rollers, and professional gamblers. The term **chip** is used by everyone else, including this book. The two terms are synonymous.

THE PERSONNEL

The Boxman

The fact that he wears a coat and tie instead of a dealer's uniform indicates that the boxman is the table supervisor. He sits at the center of the table with stacks of chips in front of him. The inside dealers are on his immediate left and right, and the stickman is directly across the table from him. When there is a big crowd at a large table, two boxmen often sit side-by-side, each one handling his end of the table.

The boxman oversees the entire game and settles any disputes that may arise. He controls the chips in the table bank and verifies that payouts by the dealers are made accurately. He also checks the dice and may disallow a bad roll of the dice.

The Inside Dealers

The double-ended craps layout requires a dealer to handle each end; thus, there are two inside dealers (sometimes called standing dealers), one at each side of the boxman. While playing craps, the inside dealer at your end of the table is the employee whom you will interact with most. The inside dealer has a number of duties:

1. This dealer handles all of your chip transactions. He will convert your cash into chips. He will also change chip denominations for you if necessary.

2. Other than for the center bets, he pays all winners and collects all losing bets.

3. He properly positions come and don't come bets as well as the place bets, and returns bets that are taken down by a player.

4. He is responsible for positioning the puck on his half of the layout.

5. He answers your questions about the various wagers.

The Stickman

Standing directly across the table from the boxman is the stickman. He is easy to spot because he is always holding a long dice stick for handling the dice. Aside from returning the dice to the shooter, the only dealings he has with the players are the handling of the center bets.

The stickman's main duty is to control the dice. He uses his stick to push a selection of dice toward a new shooter so that the shooter can choose two of them for his come-out roll. After each throw, he slides the dice back to the center of the table and announces the number that was rolled, along with some appropriate comment about the result. He waits until everyone has placed their new wagers and then pushes the pair of dice over to the shooter.

A good stickman will maintain a continuous stream of patter to liven up the game. If a 7 is rolled on the come-out, he may say, "Seven, winner on the pass line, pass line bettors win." After announcing the result of a roll, he will often encourage players to place bets that are favorable for the house, such as the field or the hardways. When a point is established, he might say something like, "Point is eight, easy eight, make your come bets."

The Floor Supervisor

The person in the pit who is observing the overall action at the craps table is the floor supervisor. His job is to extend credit and to keep track of the betting levels of various players so he has a basis for giving out comps. He also keeps an eye out for cheating and other irregularities.

The Pit Boss

At the top of the pecking order in a craps pit is the pit boss. The pit boss watches the floor supervisor, who watches the boxman, who watches the dealers, who watch the players.

OBJECT OF THE GAME

Craps players have many betting options. They may bet with the dice, against the dice, or they may bet for or against particular numbers coming up. The person throwing the dice must make a line bet for or against the dice. For purposes of this brief description, it will be assumed that the **shooter** is betting with the dice, which is the usual case. This bet is called a pass-line wager because the shooter is betting that the dice will **pass**. A line bet against the dice is called a don't-pass wager, although it is rarely referred to as a line bet.

BEAT THE CRAPS TABLE

Each hand in a game of craps has two phases: the come-out phase and the point phase. The initial roll of the dice in a hand is called the **come-out**. The number that appears on that first roll produces one of the three following results:

1. If the number is a 7 or 11, which is called a **natural**, the pass-line bettor wins immediately and the hand is over. The next roll is a new come-out.

2. If the number is a 2, 3, or 12, which is called **craps**, the pass-line bettor loses immediately and the hand is over. The next roll is a new come-out.

3. If the number is any one of the remaining numbers (4, 5, 6, 8, 9, or 10), it is called **the point**. There is, at this roll, no win/lose resolution for line bets, and the hand continues.

When a point is established at the come-out, the hand enters the point phase. Now, the shooter's goal is to repeat the point number before rolling a 7. If the point appears first, it is called **making the point**, and the pass wager wins. If the 7 is rolled before the point is repeated, it is called **sevening-out**, and the pass wager loses. Although other bets can be made on any of the numbers, in terms of the pass wager, the point and the 7 are the only numbers that have any meaning and the hand proceeds until one of those numbers appears on the dice.

Thus, a **hand**, which is sometimes called a *game* or a *round*, always begins with a come-out roll. If, on the come-out, a natural or craps is rolled, the hand is terminated, since an immediate win/lose decision has been made for the line bets. If a point number is rolled, the hand enters the point phase and remains there for as many rolls of the dice as it takes to make the point or seven-out. After making the point or sevening-out, the next roll of the dice is a new come-out that begins a new hand.

While the shooter is rolling the dice, either during the come-out or while attempting to repeat the point, there are dozens of other wagers that can be made for or against specific numbers or groups of numbers. Some of these wagers are good and some are strictly sucker bets, but all of them will be described in full detail, later on.

THE SHOOTER

The **shooter** is the player who throws the dice. Every other player wins or loses according to the number that appears on the dice, regardless of who threw them. The dice move around the table in a clockwise direction, so that everyone gets a turn to shoot. Whenever a player is offered the dice, he may either shoot them or give them up to the player on his left. There is no particular advantage or disadvantage to shooting the dice and there is no stigma attached to relinquishing them.

Before a shooter first rolls the dice, and before every succeeding come-out, he is required to make a line bet, which may be either a pass or don't pass wager.

It is rare for a shooter to make a don't pass wager because most people don't want to bet against themselves. Consequently, some confirmed don't pass bettors will give up their turn to shoot the dice.

A new shooter has to select a pair of dice from the several, usually five or six, that the stickman offers. The shooter, after placing his line bet, must then throw the dice so that they both bounce against the farthest wall of the table. Requiring the dice to bounce against the wall is to assure a random throw. If one or both dice don't bounce, the boxman has the option of declaring a bad roll by calling out, "No roll." In that case, all bets are off. A shooter who persistently underthrows the dice may lose his turn.

BEAT THE CRAPS TABLE

Should one of the dice land on a top rail or bounce clean off the table, it is automatically considered a bad roll and all bets are off. If one of the dice ends up leaning against a chip or against the table wall, the number counted is the one showing on the most horizontal surface. In most cases, the actual criterion used by the boxman is that he imagines how the dice would fall if the obstacle were removed.

If a point was established on the come-out roll, the shooter's turn continues until he sevens out. That is, he cannot lose his turn on the come-out and continues to shoot so long as he keeps making his points. However, he may give up the dice voluntarily at any time that he has not established a new point, such as right before a new come-out. The only time a shooter must give up the dice is when he sevens out while trying to make his point. The dice then pass to the player on his left.

Other than the clockwise rotation of the dice, there is no further protocol for determining the next shooter. Thus, a new player may select any open spot and step up to a table, even if that makes him the next shooter.

THE COME-OUT ROLL

As previously explained, a craps round consists of a come-out and a point phase. The start of every craps sequence is the **come-out** roll. If a natural (7 or 11) or craps (2, 3, or 12) is rolled on the come-out, the round is concluded and there is no point phase. Any other number appearing on the come-out establishes a point, and the round continues into the point phase (see the following section).

When a natural (7 or 11) is rolled on the come-out, all players who bet that the dice will pass (made a pass-line bet) immediately win their bets, while players who bet against the shooter (made a don't-pass bet) lose. When craps (2, 3, or 12) is rolled on the come-out, the reverse is true: all pass-line bettors lose and all don't-pass bettors win (except that the 12 is a push, which will be explained later). The winning line wagers are paid even money.

If a shooter rolls craps during the come-out, he retains possession of the dice. To lose the dice, a shooter has to first enter the point phase of the hand by rolling a point number, and then has to seven-out while attempting to repeat the point.

A Note on Terminology: To a craps dealer, the term "natural" means any number that resolves the line bets on a come-out roll: a 2, 3, 7, 11, or 12. To most players, the term means a pass on the come-out, a 7 or 11. Most authors of craps books also define a natural as a 7 or 11. To avoid confusion, this book will use this definition.

THE POINT PHASE

When any number other than a natural or craps is rolled on the come-out, that number becomes the point. The point number may be a 4, 5, 6, 8, 9, or 10. When one of these numbers is rolled on the come-out, the line bettors neither win nor lose; their bets are unresolved and remain in place on the layout.

For a pass-line bettor to win during the point phase, the established point number has to appear a second time before a 7 is rolled. Thus, it may take only one or two rolls, or it may take many, many rolls of the dice to resolve the line bets by repeating the point or tossing a 7. During this time, any other numbers that appear have no effect on the status of the line wagers. If a 7 appears before the point is repeated, the pass-line bettors lose. If the point is thrown before a 7 appears, the pass-line bettors win. Since either repeating the point or rolling a 7 decides the line bets, that is the end of the round.

BEAT THE CRAPS TABLE

For example, if the first roll is a 3, the pass-line bettors lose, but the shooter retains the dice and throws another come-out. If the second come-out is a 6, that becomes the point. Should the third roll be another 3, the only winners would be a field bet or a bet on 3 (which will be explained later), but the 3 has no effect on the pass-line wagers. A fourth roll of 6 makes the point and the pass-line bettors win.

After winning the first point, the same shooter now rolls a 9 for new come-out point. Then, after rolling a 2 and a 10, neither of which affect the line bets, the shooter rolls a 7. The pass-line bettors lose and the shooter loses possession of the dice.

BASIC CRAPS SUMMARY

- First roll by a new shooter is the come-out roll.
- If the come-out is a 7 or 11, pass-line bettors win.
- If the come-out is 2, 3, or 12, pass-line bettors lose.
- A come-out of 4, 5, 6, 8, 9, or 10 is the point.
- On subsequent rolls, if the point is repeated before a 7 appears, pass-line bettors win.
- If a 7 appears first, pass-line bettors lose.

3

PLAYING IN THE CASINO

SELECTING A TABLE

Just as with any other casino game, it is important that you select a table with reasonable care. Stepping up to a table and throwing out your money without first checking the limits and playing conditions may seem like a cool move, but it is a move that could be expensive.

Table Limits

Except for downtown Las Vegas where some casinos will still take a $1 bet, craps tables usually have a minimum limit of at least $5. Know ahead of time how much you intend to wager and find a table with appropriate limits. If you can't find a table with a low enough limit to fit your playing budget, go to another casino. Playing at a limit higher than you intended can be financially disastrous.

Table Ambience

Before putting your chips down at any craps table, stand back and watch the action for a few minutes. The table should feel comfortable to you and not so crowded that you would have to squeeze into a small space. Unless you are there to watch the people instead of betting and winning, avoid a table populated with overbearing and obnoxious characters. If you are a pass line bettor, be sure that the dice aren't running cold. If you intend to try your hand at don't betting, be sure the dice aren't obviously hot.

OBTAINING CHIPS AND CREDIT

Although you can place a bet with cash, the casino prefers that you use chips. To get chips, put your money on the table in front of a dealer and tell him what denominations you want. Don't drop a $100 bill on the table and ask for $50 in chips and $50 change. A casino craps table does not deal in cash—all cash is shoved into a slot in front of the boxman and drops into a strongbox that is mounted under the table. If you have a $100 bill and want only $50 in chips, go to the cashier's cage where they will accommodate you.

If you need to change the denomination of chips you already have, put them near the dealer and ask for a color change. You should never hand money or chips directly to a dealer, and he will never hand chips directly to you. By first placing the money or chips on the table, the surveillance camera can properly monitor the transaction. Be careful, however, not to toss your chips onto the table so they get mixed with other chips already there.

The craps table has grooves on the top rail where you can store your chips. It is your responsibility to protect your own chips. Just as there are occasional pickpockets, there are people around who watch for inattentive players and will swipe unmonitored chips. Be sure to guard your chips just as if they were real money, which they are. When you are finished playing, you can convert your chips back to currency at the cashier's cage.

If you are a serious player and would rather not carry around large sums of cash, you may wish to establish a line of credit at the casino. To obtain credit, you first have to stop at the cashier's cage and get rated. You will have to fill out a credit application, so they can check your credit history. If you already have credit at another casino, it won't take very long because all casinos use the same credit agency. If you have never established credit at a casino before, they will have to check with your bank, which could take a day or two—and even longer on a weekend. In any case, the casino is not likely to give you more credit than 75% of your average checking account balance because they expect you to settle any losses before you leave by writing a check.

THE WAGERS

There are over three-dozen different wagers that can be made in a casino craps game. Some of these bets are pretty good, some are not very good, and some are terrible. An overview of the various craps wagers is given below. Later on, these wagers are described in considerable detail so that you can tell the good from the bad.

Pass Bet

This is not only the most fundamental wager on the craps table, but with a house edge of 1.41% most players consider it the best bet. The pass bet, which is made immediately prior to a come-out roll, is a bet that the dice will pass (win). It is called a contract bet because it cannot be removed until it is either won or lost. A 7 or 11 rolled on the come-out is a pass bet winner, while the 2, 3, and 12 are losers. Any other number is the point, which has to be repeated before a 7 appears for the pass bet to win. After the come-out roll, an additional odds bet can be taken. These details are described in the chapter on pass wagers.

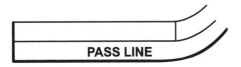

THE PASS LINE

Come Bet

Except for the timing, a come bet is similar to a pass wager. It is also a contract bet and can be made at any time except before a come-out. It is called a **contract bet** because it cannot be removed. This results in a different point (than for the pass bet) being established, which has to be repeated before a 7 appears in order to win. Like the pass bet, the first roll of a come bet is won if a 7 or 11 appears, and is lost if a 2, 3, or 12 appears. Any other number is the point for that come bet. Odds can also be taken on a come bet.

Don't Pass Bet

This is essentially the opposite of a pass bet; it is a bet against the dice. It loses when the pass bet wins and it wins when the pass bet loses, except that the 12 is a push. That is what is meant on the layout where it says "Bar 12." The reason for this is explained later in the chapter on don't pass wagers. An odds bet is also allowed on a don't pass wager.

THE DON'T PASS LINE

Don't Come Bet

The don't come bet loses when a come bet made at the same time wins; it wins when the come bet loses, except that the 12 is a push. An odds bet can be added to a don't come wager.

Place Bet

This wager is very similar to a pass bet, except that there is no come-out and the point is chosen by the bettor. When you make this wager, you are betting that the place number you bet on is rolled before a 7. The choice of numbers are the ones in the six place number boxes on the layout, namely, 4, 5, 6, 8, 9, and 10. **Buy bets** and **lay bets** are versions of place bets that are explained later in the chapter on place bets.

PLACE NUMBER BOXES

Field Bet

This wager, which is displayed prominently across the layout, covers the numbers 2, 3, 4, 9, 10, 11, and 12 in a single bet. The field bet is a **one-roll bet** that one of these numbers will appear at the next roll of the dice. If one of the four missing numbers, 5, 6, 7, or 8, is rolled, you lose the bet. This is not a good bet because the losing numbers are much more likely to appear.

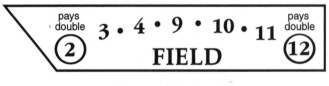

THE FIELD WAGER BOX

Big 6 and Big 8 Bets

Most craps layouts have two boxes at each end marked BIG 6 and BIG 8. A wager in one of these boxes means you are betting that a 6 (or 8) will appear before 7. If you win, the bet pays even money, which isn't enough to make it a fair bet.

THE BIG 6 AND BIG 8 BOXES

Proposition Bets

These are mainly long-shot bets with high payoffs, which is why many players make them. The prop bets are all located in the center section of the layout and are controlled by the stickman. You simply toss him your chips and tell him which bet to put them on, and if you're a winner, he pays you. The house edge for these bets ranges from 9.1% to 16.7%, which makes them the worst bets on the craps layout.

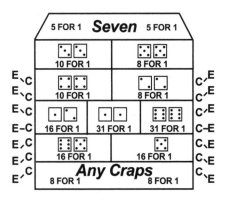

THE CENTER BETS

PLACING BETS

There are three ways to place a wager. The method you should choose depends on the bet. Some bets are positioned by the player, some by the inside dealer, and some by the stickman, and you should know which is which.

Bets Placed by Player

The player positions all wagers from the COME box down to the PASS LINE. These bets include pass, don't pass, come, don't come, field, big 6, and big 8. They are the only bets on the layout that can be set up by a player without the assistance of a dealer or stickman.

Bets Placed by Dealer

All wagers above the COME box, which are primarily the place bets, are set up by the inside dealer. Once come bets and don't come bets have been moved to a number box by the dealer, the player may not touch them. These boxes are controlled by the dealer so he can position the chips in such a way that he knows who made the bet.

Bets Placed by Stickman

The stickman controls and pays off all the wagers in the center section. These bets include the hardways and one-roll proposition bets.

Call Bets

A **call bet** is when you tell a dealer what you want to bet, but, for one reason or another, there are no chips on the table. On some layouts there is a printed rule that says *No Call Bets*, which means that bets expressed vocally only are not allowed—the chips have to be on the table. This rule, however, is not strictly enforced. You might, for example, throw down a $100 bill, telling the dealer you want to put $10 on the pass line. If the dealer doesn't have enough time to obtain the chips from the boxman and verify the count before the come-out roll, he will say, "You're covered." After the dice are rolled, he will give you your chips plus any winnings or subtract $10 from your change if the bet lost.

Taking Down Bets

Should you change your mind about a bet that has not yet been resolved (has not yet won or lost), and would like to remove it, simply ask the dealer to "take down my bet." You are allowed to take down any bets on the layout except the pass or the come bets. Pass and come bets are contract wagers that have to remain in effect until they are resolved. There are no restrictions, however, on removing any odds bets that you may have added to your pass or come wagers.

Turning Bets OFF and ON

If you want to temporarily call off a bet, instead of taking it down, you may ask the dealer to turn it off, and at a later time ask him to turn it on again. When you ask for a bet to be turned off, be sure the dealer heard your request by checking that he placed an OFF button on top of your bet. Then, when you want it to be active again, tell the dealer and he will remove the OFF button. Most wagers on the layout can be turned off so that they are not working. The only exceptions are the pass line and come bets.

Pressing Bets

If you have just won a bet and you want the winnings to ride, tell the dealer to "press my bet." He will interpret this to mean that you want to double your bet, so he will add an equal amount of your winnings to your original bet and return the difference to you. For instance, if you won a $10 place bet on the 9, the payoff is $14. The dealer will add $10 to your original bet and return $4 to you.

ROLLING THE DICE

As explained earlier, every player has the right to throw the dice when it is their turn. Possession of the dice rotates clockwise around the table, and if a player declines to roll, the dice are passed to the next player in the rotation. All players at the table win or lose their bets according to the numbers that appear on the dice, regardless of who the shooter was.

After the shooter makes the required line wager, the stickman will offer him five or six dice, from which he has to select two. Both dice must then be thrown together so that they strike the far wall of the table. The stickman announces the number that was rolled and slides the dice to the center of the table. After the bets are settled and new bets are made, the stickman slides the same two dice back over to the shooter, so that the shooter can roll again. The hand continues in this manner until the shooter sevens out. Then the dice are offered to a new shooter.

Tossing the dice is not difficult. Simply pick them up *with one hand* and lob them in a shallow arc toward the far wall of the table. Do not use two hands or you may be suspected of switching dice. For the same reason, do not rub the dice against any part of your body or your clothing. Always keep the dice in plain view. These handling rules are for the protection of all the players.

The casino wants the dice to strike the far wall of the table to assure a random throw. If they don't reach the wall, the shooter will be gently admonished, but the roll will usually stand. If it happens a second time, the roll will probably be disallowed by the boxman. You'll know this when he says, "No roll—all bets off."

Often, on his next turn, a new player who was admonished for a short roll will now throw the dice too hard so that one or both may bounce off the table. When this happens, the stickman will offer up the remaining dice so that the shooter can select two new ones. At this point, one or more players may call out, "Same dice." These superstitious players are asking you to request the same dice as the ones you had been rolling. Unless you are also superstitious, I recommend you don't do it because it will only hold up the game. Before the dice can be returned to you, the boxman has to first verify the logo and the serial numbers, and then has to check them very carefully for balance and other characteristics to be sure that misspotted or loaded dice weren't switched in. This process may take several minutes, during which time the game is stopped.

A good way to toss the dice is to visualize a coffee mug or a small cereal dish sitting on the table about a foot in front of the far wall. You try to lob (not too high) the dice into the dish without bouncing them out. By doing this, the toss will be easy enough not to leave the table, but will still have enough forward momentum to hit the wall.

TABLE ETIQUETTE

In the game of craps, there are several things to consider when it comes to table etiquette. The main thing is to avoid any action that might interfere with the shooter or slow down the flow of the game. Also very important is to avoid doing or saying anything that could upset other players. Craps players tend to be superstitious, especially the old-timers, and there are certain protocols that you need to be aware of. To keep from being reproved by a dealer or getting nasty stares from other players, be sure you remember the following rules.

Don't Rely on the Dealer
Before you step up to a table, know what you are doing. Although the dealer can be very helpful, don't depend on or expect his help, especially at a crowded table.

Try to Be Reasonably Neat
Don't put your drink on the table or drop cigarette ashes on the felt. There is a shelf under the chip rack for those items.

Keep Your Opinions to Yourself
Be friendly and enthusiastic, but avoid interacting with players you do not know. Do not give advice or criticize someone's bets or betting style.

Buy in at the Appropriate Time
The best time to buy in or change color is right after the bets from the last roll are paid and before the stickman slides the dice to the shooter. At any other time, you will probably be ignored because you are interfering with the game. The worst time to buy in is when the stickman asks if you wish to shoot. Fumbling through your wallet, you pull out some bills, and wait until the boxman counts your money. This stalls the game.

Make Your Bets Promptly

The time to bet is when the dice are sitting in front of the boxman and the stickman calls out, "Place your bets." If you wait until the stickman gives the dice to the shooter, your bet may be disallowed. You'll know this when you hear, "No bet." When there is money involved, there can be no ambiguity on a bet—every wager has to be clear and understandable.

Don't Interfere with the Shooter

When the stickman slides the dice over to the shooter, get your hands out of the table. Have your bets down before the shooter is given the dice. If the dice hit your hand and the result is a seven-out, guess who gets blamed? YOU! You can argue all you want that all you did was randomize the throw a little more, but all the hostility will still be directed at you.

Don't Interact with the Shooter

The other players will always perceive anything you do to distract the shooter, such as touching or talking, in a negative way. They believe anything that breaks the shooter's concentration can result in a bad roll. This includes any form of encouragement or a request for a particular number.

Never Say Seven

Never utter the word "seven," especially after the come-out. It is considered bad form and bad luck. Since most players will lose if a seven is rolled after the come-out, it is an unmentionable number.

Don't Hold up the Game

Throw the dice as soon as you get them. Don't waste time fiddling with them. Don't turn around and announce to your friends what number you are going to roll. This is not about you—there are other players at the table who are invested in this round. If the stickman urges, "Please pick up the dice and shoot them," he's acting for everyone at the table.

Hit the Far Wall

You may get away with a short roll once, but you will be requested to hit the wall the next time you throw. The casino wants to assure everyone that the roll is random and that they are running an honest game. Throw hard enough to reach the wall, but don't throw so hard that the dice knock down stacks of chips or bounce out of the table.

Keep a Low Profile when Making Don't Bets

Above all, keep your mouth shut. Remember, you are (seemingly) betting against most players at the table, even though you are really betting against the house.

TIPPING

Let me say at the outset that I don't believe in tipping unless a service has been rendered in an efficient and pleasant manner. In a casino, tipping is never required. You are in complete control as to when, where, and how much to tip.

In a restaurant, the tipping situation is well defined. The 15 to 20% tip has become so standardized that many patrons leave 15 or 20% whether the service was good, bad, or mediocre. In a casino, however, there are large gray areas. These gray areas are so prevalent that many people over-tip when tipping isn't even indicated.

When it comes to casino dealers, the terminology changes so that a tip becomes a **toke**. Something many people are unaware of is that if you give a craps dealer a generous toke, that toke will be shared with the other craps dealers on that shift. To comply with IRS regulations, the tokes are usually pooled and taxes withheld by the casino before the remaining money is divided among the other dealers. So your big toke is first taxed and then the balance is split up evenly between all the craps dealers in that pit.

PLAYING IN THE CASINO

Since tipping is strictly optional, why would you toke the craps dealers? As employees of the casino, you would expect them to look out for the interest of the casino before they look out for yours. Actually, craps dealers look out for your interest first, letting the pit supervisors take care of the casino. They do this because they earn a relatively low base wage and are heavily dependent on tokes from satisfied customers.

Craps dealers like to see players win because that usually means more money for them. In fact, the players often pay them more than the casino does, so it is not surprising that their loyalty is with the players. But what about the **stiffs**—those players who don't tip? Well, they do get adequate service, but they rarely get any extra help.

Inexperienced players, however, need all the help they can get. Thus, if you are a newbie, toking a dealer early on will demonstrate that you are not a stiff, and will usually assure you of getting good advice. I would also toke a dealer after a run of good luck, but only if he were a pleasant, helpful person and if I enjoyed playing at his table. Toking often pays for itself, especially if the dealer gives you some helpful advice or points out a betting mistake that would have cost you money.

There are differences of opinion as to how a toke should be presented at the craps table. The common way is to add an extra bet to whatever you are already betting on. Just put the chip next to your bet and say that it is "for the dealers." Don't use the phrase "for the boys" because nowadays many craps dealers are female. You can also ask the dealer where he would like you to bet the toke, or you can give it to him directly, which is also acceptable.

4

UNDERSTANDING THE ODDS

Craps is a game of dice combinations and odds. To figure the odds on any craps bet, you have to be thoroughly familiar with all the dice combinations and the number of ways to make each number. Until you have a full understanding of the odds for or against making the various bets, you will be at a major disadvantage while playing the game. Before you decide to skip this chapter, you should at least scan the following pages so that you know what they contain. When you read through the rest of the book, you can refer back for specific explanations on odds and combinations as you need them.

THE DICE COMBINATIONS

Craps is played with a pair of standard six-sided dice. Each of the six sides has one or more spots representing the numbers 1 through 6. Thus, each of the dice can be rolled in six different ways: 1 is the lowest number and 6 is the highest. When two dice are rolled, the spots on the uppermost surfaces are totaled together to obtain the final number; the lowest is 2, and the highest is 12. The total number of combinations that can be produced by two dice is 36.

Although one pair of dice can produce the numbers 2 through 12, the probability of rolling each of these numbers is not the same. The following diagram gives the different possible ways each number can be rolled, which is the basis for figuring the probabilities in craps.

UNDERSTANDING THE ODDS

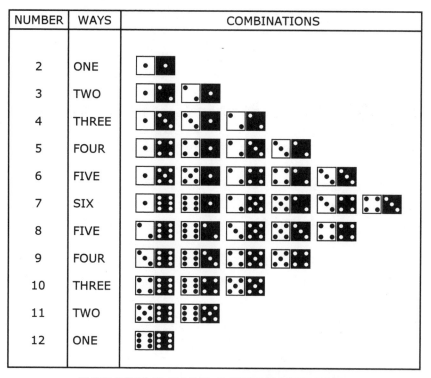

NUMBER	WAYS	COMBINATIONS
2	ONE	
3	TWO	
4	THREE	
5	FOUR	
6	FIVE	
7	SIX	
8	FIVE	
9	FOUR	
10	THREE	
11	TWO	
12	ONE	

POSSIBLE DICE COMBINATIONS

Of the many combinations that can be made by the two dice, some numbers are more likely to appear than others. For instance, a 2 can be made only when both dice show a single spot, and a 12 can only be made with a 6+6. On the other hand, a seven can be made with 1+6, 2+5, 3+4, 4+3, 5+2, and 6+1, a total of six different ways.

Some people have the mistaken belief that a 7 can only be made three ways: 1+6, 2+5, and 3+4. They don't take into account that the numbers on the two dice can be reversed, which produces three additional ways. To make this clearer in the above diagram, each pair of dice is shown as one black and one white. In this way, it is more obvious that a 1+6, for example, can also be rolled as a 6+1.

Remembering the Combinations

When you examine the chart of dice combinations, note the symmetry on either side of the 7. The number of ways to roll a 6 is the same as an 8; a 5 is the same as a 9; and a 4 is the same as a 10. Furthermore, if you look at the numbers 7 and below, the ways to roll are exactly one less than the number itself. In other words, a 2 can be rolled one way, a 3 can be rolled two ways, a 4 can be rolled three ways, on up to a 7, which can be rolled six different ways. The numbers higher than 7 are simply the complements of the lower numbers. For instance, the 4 and 10 can each be rolled three different ways: 1+3, 2+2, and 3+1 for a 4, and 4+6, 5+5, and 6+4 for a 10.

Now, if you memorize the five symmetrical pairs: 2-12, 3-11, 4-10, 5-9, and 6-8, you can easily remember the ways to roll any number. It is always one less than the lower of the complementary pair.

THE MEANING OF ODDS

The statistical term for describing the chance of an event occurring is **probability**. The beauty of this term is that it is not ambiguous. It is always a single number between 0 and 1 that can be stated as a fraction or a decimal. Sometimes the decimal is multiplied by 100 and expressed as a percentage. A probability of 0 means that a particular event never occurs, a probability of 0.5 means that the event is likely to occur half the time, and a probability of 1 means that the event occurs all the time.

Most gamblers, however, prefer to use the term **odds**. The problem with this term is that it can be stated in several different ways, leading to confusion and misinterpretation by newcomers. The confusion arises from the use of the modifiers *against*, *to*, *for*, and *in*.

As an example, for a single six-sided cube, there is one way to roll any particular number and there are five ways to not get that number. If you are betting that a 4 appears on the next roll, there is one way to win and five ways to lose. The total number of possibilities is six, which is the sum of the ways to win and the ways to lose. This situation can be described in the following ways:

- The odds of winning are 1 *in* 6. This means that there is 1 chance of winning out of a possible 6 chances.
- The odds *for* winning are 1 *to* 5. This means that there is 1 chance of winning and 5 chances of losing.
- The odds *against* winning are 5 *to* 1. This means that there are 5 chances of losing and 1 chance of winning.

In the first of the above examples, a fraction bar can be substituted for the word "in." For instance, 1 in 6 is often written as 1/6. In the second case, a colon can be substituted for the word "to." For instance, 1 to 5 is often written as 1:5.

No matter how they are stated, the above are all mathematical ratios. You must be careful, however, to ascertain what the ratio is. In particular, be sure you know if the ratio is chances of winning vs. chances of losing or if the ratio is chances of winning vs. all possible chances (winning plus losing).

Figuring the Odds

With a pair of dice, there are a total of 36 possible combinations, so the ways of making and not making a particular number on a single roll have to add up to 36. Since there are four ways to make a 5, there are 32 ways of not making a 5 (36 minus 4). That means the odds of rolling a 5 are 4 in 36, and the odds against rolling a 5 are 32 to 4, or 8 to 1. The odds against making any other number is figured in the same way. The results are shown in the following chart.

ODDS ON THE NEXT ROLL			
Number	**Ways to Roll**	**Odds**	**Odds Against**
2	1	1 in 36	35 to 1
3	2	1 in 18	17 to 1
4	3	1 in 12	11 to 1
5	4	1 in 9	8 to 1
6	5	5 in 36	6.2 to 1
7	6	1 in 6	5 to 1
8	5	5 in 36	6.2 to 1
9	4	1 in 9	8 to 1
10	3	1 in 12	11 to 1
11	2	1 in 18	17 to 1
12	1	1 in 36	35 to 1

To figure the odds of rolling any one of a group of numbers, add together the ways all of the desired numbers can be rolled to determine the number of ways to win. For instance, to win on the come-out, you have to roll a 7 or 11. Since a 7 can be made six ways and an 11 can be made two ways, there are eight ways to win and 28 ways (36 minus 8) to roll craps or a point. Thus, the odds of winning on the come-out are 8 in 36, or 1 in 4. The odds against winning on the come-out are 28 to 8, or 7 to 2, or 3.5 to 1.

Payoff Odds

This discussion, so far, has been about **true odds** or **correct odds**. When a casino pays off a winning bet, however, they don't pay correct odds because they expect to make a profit. Instead, they pay **house odds**, which are slightly poorer than the true odds. The difference is the **house edge**.

For example, when you make a place bet that a 4 will appear before a 7, there are six ways to roll a 7 and three ways to roll a 4. Thus, the correct odds are 6 to 3, which is the same as 2 to 1. If you win, the casino will only pay you 9 to 5 odds (instead of 10 to 5, which would be 2 to 1) resulting in a house edge of 6.7%.

On a craps layout, you will often see a payoff stated as 5 *for* 1 instead of 5 *to* 1. On a 5 to 1 payoff, if you wager $5 and win, you will be paid $25 *and* get to keep your original $5 bet. If the payoff is stated as 5 *for* 1, you will also be paid $25, but will lose your original bet. In other words, the casino gives you $25 *for* your $5. By simply changing the word "to" to the word "for", the casino gets $5 more from you.

Showing a payoff as 5 for 1 is a ploy to make it appear more generous than at a less deceptive casino where the payoff for the same bet is stated as 4 to 1. Although this trickery doesn't fool professionals, it can easily mislead the casual gambler.

5

THE PASS LINE AND COME WAGERS

The line bets are those based on the fundamental premise of the game of craps, in which the shooter establishes a point and then tries to repeat it before rolling a 7. The two line bets are called the pass and the don't pass wagers. This chapter explains the pass bet, while the don't pass bet is covered in the next chapter. Also covered in this chapter is the come wager, which is very similar to the pass bet, and the taking of odds, which is an add-on bet to the pass and come wagers. These wagers are the best bets on the table in terms of low house advantage.

THE PASS LINE WAGER

The **pass line** wager is the most fundamental bet on any craps table. A person making a pass wager is betting that the shooter makes his point. He would also win if the shooter rolled a 7 or 11 on the come-out, and lose if he rolled a 2, 3, or 12. A winning pass bet pays even money, meaning that for a $10 bet, the winner gets to keep his $10 bet and is paid an additional $10.

The pass bet is the most popular bet made by craps players, and for good reason. Most of the time it is the best bet on the layout, and it has a very low house advantage of 1.41%. Taking the odds bet, which is explained later in this chapter can reduce this low advantage even further.

A pass bet should be made just before a come-out roll, that is, when the black side of the puck is facing up. To make the bet, put your chip or chips on the pass line, which runs the full length of both the left and right betting sections on the layout (see illustration). You can make a pass bet after the come-out, but then it is no longer a good bet because the best odds of winning occur on the come-out roll.

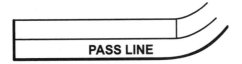

THE PASS LINE

WHAT IS A PUT BET?

A late pass bet (one made after the come-out) actually has a name: it is called a **put bet**. Although most dealers will warn you against this, some casinos love put bettors because the house edge is 9.1% on a point of 6 or 8, 20% on a point of 5 or 9, or a whopping 33% on a point of 4 or 10. On a point of 4 or 10, you would have to take at least 20x odds to reduce the house edge to anywhere close to a pass bet with no odds. This is undoubtedly the dumbest bet in craps.

Since there are six ways to make a 7, and two ways to make an 11, the chances of winning on the come-out are 8 out of 36. By the same reasoning, there are 4 chances out of 36 that craps will be rolled. Thus, on the come-out, the likelihood of winning is twice as good as losing. The rest of the time, 24 chances out of 36, a point will be established, and the round continues.

Once the point is established, the chance of winning a pass

bet drops considerably. This is because a 7 can be made six different ways while any of the point numbers are less than that, as the following chart shows.

ODDS OF REPEATING THE POINT BEFORE ROLLING A SEVEN			
Point	Ways to Roll the Point	Ways to Roll a Seven	Odds
4	3	6	1 to 2
5	4	6	2 to 3
6	5	6	5 to 6
8	5	6	5 to 6
9	4	6	2 to 3
10	3	6	1 to 2

Thus, it would seem logical to remove your pass bet after the come-out, but the casino will not allow you to do that. A pass bet is a contract wager, and once it is made, it has to remain until it wins or loses.

THE COME WAGER

Some craps players are confused about the **come** wager, and shouldn't be. The come bet is very easy to understand because, except for the timing, it is identical to the pass wager. The come bet can be made at any time *except* before a come-out roll, that is, a come bet can be made any time a pass bet is not normally made. When a come bet is made, the very next roll acts as a come-out for that come bet, independent of what is happening with the pass bets.

In other words, by placing a come bet, any roll can become a come-out for that bet, and the same rules apply as for a pass bet. You can make as many or as few come bets as you wish.

THE PASS LINE AND COME WAGERS

In this way, you can make bets on additional points while the pass line shooter is trying to repeat his original point. Thus, depending on how many come bets you make, you can have two or more points working at the same time.

Just as with a pass bet, if the first roll after placing the come bet is a 7 or 11, the come bet wins. And if it is a 2, 3, or 12, it loses. Any other number becomes the point for your come bet, which has to be repeated before a 7 appears in order to win. When it wins, a come bet pays even money, just like a pass bet. Not surprisingly, the casino's edge on a come bet is 1.41%, exactly the same as for a pass bet. The house edge can be reduced dramatically by taking odds, as explained in the next section.

To make a come bet, place your chip or chips in the big COME box, which you should do only when the white side of the puck is facing up. If the next roll is not a natural (which you would win) or craps (which you would lose), then it is your come point and the dealer will move your bet to the appropriate numbered box. This is so both you and the dealer know which number has to be repeated for you to win the come bet. Now the only numbers that have meaning on the succeeding rolls are a 7 (you lose) or your come point (you win). As you can see, this is exactly the same as making a pass bet, except that the point is a different number.

When you win your come point, the dealer will move your original bet back into the COME box and stack the winnings alongside. It is then your responsibility to retrieve the chips, or they will be considered a new come wager. Once made, you cannot take down or turn off a come bet. Just as for a pass bet, the come bet is a contract wager that must remain until it wins or loses.

As an aid in understanding come wagers, the following example shows how the pass bets and come bets are handled during a typical sequence of rolls:

Action: The player makes a bet on the pass line.

The come-out roll is a 9. A point of 9 is established and the dealer moves the puck to the 9 box with the white ON side facing up.

Action: The player now places a bet in the come box.

The first point roll is a 4. A point of 4 is established for the come bet and the dealer moves the bet to the 4 box. The pass bet is unaffected.

The second point roll is another 4. *The come bet wins* and the player is paid for the come bet. The pass bet is unaffected.

Action: The player makes a new come bet.

The third point roll is a 5. A point of 5 is established for the come bet and the dealer moves the bet to the 5 box. The pass bet is unaffected.

The fourth point roll is a 9. *The pass bet wins* and the player is paid for the pass bet. The dealer moves the puck out of the 9 box and turns the black OFF side up. This ends the sequence and the next roll is a come-out. The come bet is unaffected by the 9. It is still waiting for either a 5 or a 7, which are now the only two numbers that have any effect on the come bet.

Action: The player makes a new pass bet.

The come-out roll is an 8. A point of 8 is established and the dealer moves the puck to the 8 box with the white ON side facing up. The come bet is unaffected.

The first point roll is a 7. *This is a seven-out and both the pass and the come bets lose.* The dealer moves the puck out of the 8 box and turns the black OFF side up. This ends the hand and the shooter loses the dice.

Action: The player makes a new pass bet.

The come-out roll is a 6. A point of 6 is established by a new shooter and the dealer moves the puck to the 6 box with the white ON side facing up.

Action: The player makes a new come bet.

The first point roll is a 7. *This is a seven-out for the pass bet and a win for the come bet. The player loses the pass bet and wins the come bet.* The dealer moves the puck out of the 6 box and turns the black OFF side up. This ends the hand and the shooter loses the dice. The next roll is a new come-out.

In the last roll of this example, the come bet won on the 7 because it was the initial roll for that come bet and a point was not yet established. Had that roll been a 2, 3, or 12, the come bet would have lost.

TAKING ODDS

The small table-limit sign on the inside wall of the craps table is the only clue to the existence of the odds bet. Beneath the table limits is a line that may say, *"Full Double Odds"* or *"3X - 4X - 5X Odds"* or some other statement that defines the maximum odds permitted at that table. There is no clue anywhere on the craps layout itself that this bet exists. When the odds bet wins, it is paid at correct odds (rather than house odds), which means that the payoff for winning is exactly the same as the risk of making the bet, leaving the house with a zero advantage. It is the best bet in the game of craps and (unless you are a blackjack card counter) is also the best bet in the casino. Accordingly, it is a very important and worthwhile wager that is necessary for every craps player to completely understand.

The odds bet is not an independent wager. It has to be made as an add-on to an existing pass-line or come wager, and is called **taking odds** on the point. The only time odds can be taken for a pass bet is after a point is established, and the bet is made by stacking additional chips behind your pass bet, as shown below. You can take odds at any time if you have a pass bet working, but it is best to do so right after the come-out.

BEAT THE CRAPS TABLE

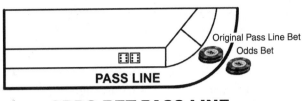

ODDS BET-PASS LINE

For a come bet, odds can only be taken after a point is established for that come bet. The odds bet can be made after the dealer moves the come bet to a point number. In this case, instead of putting the chips behind the come bet, they should be given to the dealer while saying, "odds on the come." The dealer will then place them on top of your come bet with an offset, so he can tell which portion of the bet is the come and which is the odds.

The payouts for the different point numbers are shown in the following chart, which is an expansion of the previous chart on pass bets.

ODDS PAID FOR EACH POINT			
Point	Ways to Roll	Odds Against	Odds Paid
4	3	2 to 1	2 to 1
5	4	3 to 2	3 to 2
6	5	6 to 5	6 to 5
8	5	6 to 5	6 to 5
9	4	3 to 2	3 to 2
10	3	2 to 1	2 to 1

As the chart shows, the mathematical odds against making a point are exactly the same as the payoff odds, giving the casino a zero advantage. Of course, the casino still has an edge on the original pass-line or come wager.

Should you have a come bet working during a new come-out, the odds portion of the bet will automatically be turned off. That means if the come bet wins (by repeating its point) or loses (by a roll of 7) during the come-out, the odds portion is unaffected and would be returned to you. This rule is designed to eliminate the conflict you would experience if you also had a pass bet working. Otherwise, if the shooter rolled a 7, you would win the pass bet, but lose the come bet with its large odds bet. If this doesn't bother you, or you didn't make a pass bet, you can ask the dealer to "keep my odds bet working," and he will place a small ON button on top of your chips.

Because the casino has no edge on the odds portion of the bet, taking odds effectively reduces the overall edge. The amount of the reduction depends on the size of the odds bet. Originally, an odds bet was restricted to the size of the pass or come bet, and this was called **single odds**. Today, almost all casinos in the United States allow **double odds**, and many offer **triple odds**. As a result of stiff competition, some casinos in Las Vegas offer 10x odds, and a few offer as much as 100x odds. Even in Atlantic City some casinos are now offering 5x and 10x odds on their $25 limit tables. The effect of the odds bet on the combined house edge for the pass line or come bet is as follows:

HOUSE EDGE FOR PASS OR COME WAGERS	
Pass Line or Come Bet	**House Edge**
With no odds	1.41%
With 1x odds	0.85%
With 2x odds	0.61%
With full double odds*	0.57%
With 3x odds	0.47%
With 3-4-5x odds*	0.37%
With 5x odds	0.33%
With 10x odds	0.18%
With 100x odds	0.02%

*See explanation in "What are Full Double Odds or 3-4-5X Odds"

The odds bet can be made for any amount up to the maximum allowed by the casino. Thus, if you made a $10 pass bet and the casino allows 3x odds, you can take any amount of odds up to a maximum of $30.

WHAT ARE FULL DOUBLE ODDS OR 3-4-5X ODDS?

Some casinos use the term **Full Double Odds**, which means that a player can take 2.5x odds on a point of 6 or 8, and 2x odds on all other points. This is done to facilitate the 6:5 payoff for a point of 6 or 8 when the amount of the bet isn't a multiple of 5. Double odds on a $12 pass bet, for instance, would be $24, which can't be paid correctly in whole dollars for a point of 6 or 8. Not wanting to deal in small change, most casinos would pay the winner $28 instead of the correct amount of $28.80. To avoid shorting the payoff, the player can bet $30 (2.5 x $12), which will then pay the winner the correct amount of $36.

When a casino uses the term **3-4-5x Odds**, it means that a maximum of 3x odds is allowable on a point of 4 or 10, 4x odds on a 5 or 9, and 5x on a 6 or 8. This is done to simplify the payouts for players who take the maximum odds. Regardless of the point, when a 3-4-5x bettor wins, the total payout (pass bet plus odds bet) will always be 7 times the amount of the pass bet. Many casinos in Las Vegas are now offering 3-4-5x odds.

Most casinos don't deal in small change and pay off only in whole dollars. To assure that you get the correct payoff when taking odds on a point of 5 or 9, the amount of the bet should be an even number. For instance, if the point is 9 and your odds bet is $15, you will be paid only $22 instead of the correct amount of $22.50. To avoid being shortchanged, your odds bet should have been either $14 or $16. The payoff odds of 3:2 can always be correctly made with whole dollars if the bet is an even number.

THE PASS LINE AND COME WAGERS

In the above example, you were likely playing at a table with triple odds and made a $5 pass bet. Now the shooter rolls a 9, so what do you do? You would like to take maximum odds, but the maximum odds bet is $15, leaving you with the potential of being shorted on the payoff. To avoid this, it is customary to just add another dollar to your bet to make it $16, which will pay off at an even $24.

The other problem is with the points 6 or 8, where the payoff is 6:5. The only way that payoff can be made correctly in whole dollars is if the bet is divisible by five. Say you are at a double odds table, the point is 8, and you want to take maximum odds on a $6 pass bet, which would be $12. You have two choices: you can either put out $10 or you can ask the dealer if you can bet $15 instead of $12. At a "full double odds" table, this is accepted procedure, but most double odds tables will allow it as well.

With odds of 2:1, the points 4 and 10 do not present a payoff problem. The payoff is simply double the amount of the bet.

6

THE DON'T PASS AND DON'T COME WAGERS

Players who make don't pass and don't come wagers are called wrong bettors because their bets are in opposition to those who make pass and come bets. Before getting into the details of these wagers, a short discussion on right and wrong bettors will be useful for understanding the don't bets.

RIGHT AND WRONG BETTORS

One of the interesting aspects of craps is that you can bet either with the shooter or against him. A player who bets that the dice will pass is sometimes called a **right bettor**, and a player who bets that the dice will not pass is sometimes called a **wrong bettor**. Thus, those players who place pass-line or come bets seem to be betting against the house. Those who make don't pass or don't come bets are wrong bettors, and seem to be betting with the house. Since the house has a built-in edge, it would appear to be better to bet with the house, however, as we will see later, the house has a slick way of compensating so that it has the edge either way.

Right and *wrong* are terms used by some gamblers with the implication that there is something bad or immoral with betting against the dice. Actually, being a wrong bettor is neither devious nor illicit; it is a legitimate betting strategy in craps. Because of the negative implication, however, casino employees use the terms **don't bettor** and **don't bet**. To the casino, everyone who places a bet is a right bettor. In this book we use the terms right or wrong as a shortcut method to indicate betting with or against the dice, with no bias either way.

Most craps players are right bettors. At any crowded craps table, you will usually find only one or two don't bettors, if any. So, why are there so few don't bettors when the house edge is essentially the same as for a right bettor? A lot of it has to do with the psychology of betting against the shooter. Furthermore, few people are willing to go up against the prevailing emotions of the crowd. It's something like cheering for your team while sitting on the wrong side of the stadium.

THE DON'T PASS WAGER

The **don't pass** bettor is hoping that the shooter does not make his point. This is the exact opposite of the pass bettor. In fact, a don't pass bet wins if the shooter rolls a 7 before repeating his point. The don't pass win pays even money, just like the pass bet.

Since everything appears to be opposite on this bet, you would expect the payouts at the come-out to be opposite. That is, the don't pass bettor should win on a 2, 3, or 12, and lose on a 7 or 11. This is almost true, but if it was exactly true, the don't pass bettor would have a mathematical edge on the house.

Since we know the casino doesn't give anything away, how does it get its advantage on don't bets? Very simply: by not paying for a 12 on the come-out. This is what is meant by the notation "BAR 12" on the don't pass line. In other words, when a 12 is rolled at the come-out, for don't pass bettors the 12 is a push rather than a win. This simple rule gives the house a 1.40% edge, which is almost identical to the edge on a pass bet.

BEAT THE CRAPS TABLE

Some casinos bar the 2 instead of the 12. It doesn't matter which of these numbers is barred because each one can be rolled only one way. If you find a casino that bars the 3, avoid making a don't bet or, better yet, leave the casino. A 3 can be made in two ways, so barring it substantially raises the house advantage on don't bets.

Just as for a pass bet, a don't pass bet must be made just before a come-out roll, that is, when the black side of the puck is facing up. To make the bet, put your chip or chips on the don't pass line, which is smaller than the pass line (see illustration) because there are far fewer don't bettors than pass bettors.

THE DON'T PASS LINE

The casino does not allow you to make a don't pass bet after the come-out because the best odds of winning occur after the come-out roll. For the same reason, the casino will not allow you to increase your don't pass bet after the come-out. You can, however, lay odds, which will be explained later in this chapter.

Since there are six ways to make a 7, plus two ways to make an 11, the chances of losing on the come-out are 8 out of 36. By the same reasoning, there are 3 chances out of 36 that a 2 or 3 will be rolled, while the 12 is a standoff. Thus, on the come-out, your chance of losing is over twice as high as winning. The rest of the time, 24 chances out of 36, a point will be established, and the sequence enters the point phase.

Once the point is established, your chance of winning increases considerably. This is because a 7, which is a winner for the don't bettor, can be made six different ways. As the following chart shows, the chance of repeating any of the point numbers is less than the possibility of rolling a 7.

ODDS OF ROLLING A 7 BEFORE REPEATING THE POINT			
Point	Ways to Roll the Point	Ways to Roll a Seven	Odds
4	3	6	2 to 1
5	4	6	3 to 2
6	5	6	6 to 5
8	5	6	6 to 5
9	4	6	3 to 2
10	3	6	2 to 1

Although the casino will allow you to remove your don't pass bet after the come-out, you would be foolish to do so. The chart clearly shows that, although your chances of winning on any point (by rolling a 7) are significantly better than even, the casino will pay you even money.

THE DON'T COME WAGER

As you have probably figured out by now, the don't come wager is the opposite of the come bet. The relationship between the don't come wager and the don't pass bet is the same as the relationship between the come wager and the pass bet. As with the come bet, the don't come bet can be made at any time except before a come-out roll, that is, a don't come bet can be made any time a don't pass bet is not normally made. When a don't come bet is made, the very next roll acts as a come-out for that don't come bet, independent of what is happening with the don't pass and pass line bets.

By placing a don't come bet, any roll (except the come-out) can establish a point for that bet, and don't pass rules apply.

You can make as many or as few don't come bets as you wish. In this way, you can make bets against additional points while the pass line shooter is trying to repeat his original point. Depending on how many don't come bets you make, you can have two or more points working at the same time.

Just as with a don't pass bet, if the first roll after placing the don't come bet is a 7 or 11, the bet loses. And if it is a 2 or 3, it wins, the 12 being a standoff. Any other number becomes the point for the don't come bet, and if a 7 appears before the point is repeated, the bet wins. When it wins, a don't come bet pays even money, just like a don't pass bet. By now, most readers already figured out that the casino's edge on a don't come bet is 1.40%, which is exactly the same as for a don't pass bet. The house edge can be reduced dramatically by laying odds, as explained in the next section.

To make a don't come bet, place your chip or chips in the small don't come box, which you should do only when the white side of the puck is facing up. If the next roll is not a 7 or 11 (which you would lose) or a 2 or 3 (which you would win), then it is your point and the dealer will move your bet to a small box above the appropriate place-number box. Now the only numbers that have meaning on the succeeding rolls are a 7 (you win) or your don't come point (you lose). As you can see, this is exactly the same as making a don't pass bet, except that the point is a different number.

LAYING ODDS

Just like the pass bettor, the don't bettor can add an odds bet to his don't pass or don't come wager. The only difference is that the pass bettor *takes* odds, meaning that if he wins, he gets paid more than the amount of his bet, whereas the don't bettor has to **lay odds** because he gets paid less than even money on the odds portion of the bet.

THE DON'T PASS AND DON'T COME WAGERS

Like pass bettors, when don't bettors win, they are paid at true odds for the odds portion of their bet. They are paid less than even money, however, because they have a better than even chance of winning the bet as the previous chart indicated. It doesn't matter whether the odds bet is made by a pass or a don't pass bettor, the house advantage is always zero, making it the best bet on the table.

Just as for pass bettors, the odds bet has to be made as an add-on to an existing don't pass or don't come wager. The only time a player can lay odds for a don't pass bet is after a point is established, and the bet is made by stacking additional chips alongside the don't pass bet. The dealer will reposition the chips, but you don't have to worry about that.

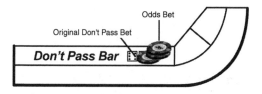

ODDS BET: DON'T PASS

For a don't come bet, you can lay odds only after a point is established for that don't come bet. The odds bet can be made after the dealer relocates the don't come bet behind the appropriate point number. Instead of putting the chips next to the don't come bet, put them in the don't come box and tell the dealer that you want to lay odds. The dealer will then place them alongside your don't come bet and **heel** the stack, so he can tell which portion of the bet is for the odds. When a stack is heeled, the bottom chip lays flat and the rest of the stack is tilted so that it is half on and half off the bottom chip.

The payouts for the different point numbers are shown in the following chart, which is an expansion of the previous chart on don't pass bets.

BEAT THE CRAPS TABLE

ODDS FOR EACH POINT			
Point	Ways to Roll	Odds Against	Odds Paid
4	3	1 to 2	1 to 2
5	4	2 to 3	2 to 3
6	5	5 to 6	5 to 6
8	5	5 to 6	5 to 6
9	4	2 to 3	2 to 3
10	3	1 to 2	1 to 2

Clearly, the mathematical odds against rolling a 7 before repeating the point are exactly the same as the payoff odds, giving the casino a zero advantage. Of course, the casino still has an edge on the original don't pass or don't come wager.

As was previously explained, if you have an active come bet working during a new come-out, in most casinos the odds portion of the bet will be off. This is not true for a don't come bet—the entire bet is working all the time. This is because there is no conflict. While the pass-line bettors are hoping for a 7 on the come-out, the don't come bettors are as well.

When laying odds, the amount you are allowed to bet depends on how much you may win, and that depends on the point. For instance, if you made a $10 don't pass or don't come bet at a full double odds table, you can lay $30 in order to win $25 for a point of 6 or 8. The rule used by the casino is that the most you can lay is the amount you would win if you took the limit on a pass bet. If you have trouble with this, the dealer will be glad to help you figure it out.

Consequently, for the same odds multiple, the amount a don't bettor is allowed to lay is always larger than the amount a pass bettor is allowed to take. This results in a stronger reduction of the combined house edge when a don't bettor lays odds, as shown in the following chart.

HOUSE EDGE FOR DON'T WAGERS	
Don't Pass or Don't Come Bet	House Edge
With no odds	1.36%
With 1x odds	0.68%
With 2x odds	0.45%
With full double odds	0.43%
With 3x odds	0.34%
With 3-4-5x odds	0.27%
With 5x odds	0.23%
With 10x odds	0.12%

The house edge calculation, of course, is based on the actual amount of money risked, not on the odds multiplier.

SPECIAL NOTE ON THE HOUSE EDGE

Granted, knowing the exact house edge down to the second decimal is not that important to the player, but you may wonder why the house edge percentages for don't wagers in the above chart are different than those published in most other craps books. This section will explain the reasons, and has been added to primarily satisfy the mathematically curious. Learning about this is not likely to make you a better craps player.

The inconsistency in the house edge for don't bets has two aspects to it, and the first concerns the basic don't wager without odds. There are two statistically-legitimate ways to calculate the edge giving different results, but the difference is not very significant. One way does not count ties (the push on the 12) and gives a value of 1.40%. The second way counts ties as a money bet (since money *is* at risk) and gives a result of 1.36%, which is the value used in this book. See the chart below.

The second aspect involves the house edge calculation for the combined don't wager and laying odds, which is a different story. It all started when I noticed a discrepancy between the numbers published by Michael Shackleford on his *The Wizard of Odds* web site and those published in all the books I had read. A discussion with Shackleford convinced me that he was right. We concluded that the numbers in most other books are clearly incorrect because they do not take into account the fact that you can bet more money laying odds than taking odds for the same odds multiple.

But, how can so many books be wrong? The numbers seemed to originate from a single seemingly authoritative source and were subsequently propagated throughout the craps literature. The most logical candidate for that source was the late John Scarne, who, at one time, was considered to be the world's foremost expert on gambling. In his 1961 book, *Complete Guide to Gambling*, he gives the incorrect numbers along with the calculations he used. This was repeated in the 1974 edition. His calculations show that he did not take into account that the most you are allowed to lay is based on how much you can win.

Since Scarne died over fifteen years ago, we cannot ask him why he did it that way. He was considered to be a good mathematician, so the error had to be a momentary lapse. He apparently never revisited the calculation, and neither did most of the subsequent gambling writers. It is not enough to say we are right and most others are wrong—we have to prove it. The proof is in the Appendix of this book, which shows the calculations and explains the mathematical basis for the numbers.

THE DON'T PASS AND DON'T COME WAGERS

HOUSE EDGE FOR DON'T WAGERS

Don't Wager	This Book	Other Books
With no odds	1.36%	1.40%
With 1x odds	0.68%	0.83%
With 2x odds	0.45%	0.59%

7

THE PLACE NUMBER WAGERS

The place number wagers consist of a variety of bets for which you can choose your own point number. They are very similar to pass-line bets, except that there is no come-out and the point has already been determined by the bettor. On the layout, the place number wagers are the six numbered boxes directly above the large COME box (see illustration). The amount of the payoff for a win depends on the point number and whether the wager was for a regular place bet, a buy bet, or a lay bet.

PLACE NUMBER BOXES

THE PLACE BET

The basic place number wager is the **place bet**. When you make this wager, you are betting that the place number you bet on will be rolled before a 7. The choice of numbers are the ones in the six place number boxes on the layout, namely, 4, 5, 6, 8, 9, and 10. Although a place bet can be made at any time, it is usually made right after a come-out roll because all place bets are turned off (not working) during a come-out.

THE PLACE NUMBER WAGERS

Winning place bets are paid off at less than true odds, giving the house a hefty edge on most of the numbers. The payoff and house edge for each number is shown on the following chart.

PLACE BET PAYOFFS			
Place Number	True Odds	Payoff Odds	House Edge
4	2 to 1	9 to 5	6.7%
5	3 to 2	7 to 5	4.0%
6	6 to 5	7 to 6	1.5%
8	6 to 5	7 to 6	1.5%
9	3 to 2	7 to 5	4.0%
10	2 to 1	9 to 5	6.7%

To make a place bet, put your chips in the Come box and tell the dealer which number or numbers you want to bet on. The dealer will then move your chips to the appropriate place number box, positioning them so that he knows which player made the bet. You should never put your chips in any of the point number boxes—only the dealer is permitted to do that.

To be assured of getting the full payoff, your bet should be in multiples of $5 for the place numbers 4, 5, 9, or 10, and should be in multiples of $6 for the 6 or 8. Otherwise, an exact payoff would involve small change. If you made a $5 bet on an 8, for example, an exact payoff would be $5.83 at 7:6 odds. Consequently, if you don't make your bet at the correct multiple, you will likely be shorted on the payoff because most craps tables do not deal in increments of less than a dollar.

When you win a place bet, the dealer will return your winnings, leaving the original wager on the layout so that you still have a bet working on that number. You can ask that your original bet be returned. Just say to the dealer, "Please take down the 8," or whatever number you are betting on.

BEAT THE CRAPS TABLE

Just as you can make a place bet at any time, you can also remove or **take down** the bet at any time. Alternately, instead of taking it down, you can ask the dealer to **turn off** your bet for one or more rolls. He will then put an OFF button on top of your chips. You can also reduce or increase your bet whenever you want to.

Place bets are popular because you don't have to wait for a number to appear twice in order to win, as you do with a pass or come bet. For instance, a $5 come bet on the 5, with $10 odds ($15 total action) will win $20 the second time the 5 appears. A $15 place bet on the 5 will win $21, and it will win the *first time* the 5 appears. The second time the 5 appears, the place bettor will be ahead $42. Of course, the place bettor loses the odds advantage of the come-out roll.

To get the most action, many of these players do not bet just one number at a time, but spread their bets over several place numbers at once. One way of doing this is by making a pass bet and then betting the place numbers across the board. Another way is to forget the pass bet, and only make place bets. The only thing you have to remember is that a bet on 4, 5, 9, or 10 has to be a multiple of $5, and a bet on 6 or 8 has to be a multiple of $6.

For example, if you bet "$32 across," you will be betting all the place numbers, and the dealer will put $5 each on the numbers 4, 5, 9, and 10, and put $6 on the 6 and the 8 ($5 + $5 + $5 + $5 + $6 + $6 = $32). If you bet "$22 inside," you will be betting all four inside numbers: 5, 6, 8, 9. If you bet "$20 outside," you will be betting all four outside numbers: 4, 5, 9, 10. The dealer will determine from the amount of money you give him, whether or not you want a duplicate bet on an established point.

THE BUY BET

A **buy bet** is simply a place bet that is paid off at the correct odds. In return for being so generous on the payoff, the casino charges a 5% commission when you win. This results in a house edge that is generally less than for regular place bets, as shown in the following chart.

ODDS PAID FOR EACH BUY NUMBER			
Number	Ways to Roll	Odds Paid	House Edge
4	3	2 to 1	1.7%
5	4	3 to 2	2.0%
6	5	6 to 5	2.3%
8	5	6 to 5	2.3%
9	4	3 to 2	2.0%
10	3	2 to 1	1.7%

To make a buy bet, give the dealer your chips and say, "I'm buying the 4," (or whatever number you are buying). The dealer will stack your bet in the 4 box and put a BUY button on top to show that it isn't a place bet. If the 4 is rolled before a 7 appears, you will be paid 2:1 odds (less 5% commission) on your bet. This is significantly better than the 9:5 odds that would have been paid if it was a place bet.

Since the minimum commission at most tables is $1, you should never bet less than $20 on a single buy bet. If, for example, you bet only $10, the $1 commission would amount to 10%. In many casinos, however, if you bet $10 on the 4 and another $10 on the 10 (at the same time), you will only be charged $1. On the other hand, a $10 buy bet on the 4 is still a better bet than an equivalent place bet. The buy bet will pay back $20 minus $1 commission for a net of $19, while the place bet pays only $18.

BEAT THE CRAPS TABLE

If you make a bet larger than $20 that is not divisible by 20, most casinos will round the commission up to the nearest dollar, if the bet is more than $25. Some casinos, however, will round down, so that you can make a larger bet and still only pay a $1 commission. Whenever you want to make a buy bet, ask the dealer how they round the commission for odd-amount bets.

Buy bets are automatically off (not working) during a come-out, unless you request otherwise. You can remove your buy bet at any time by asking the dealer to, "take down my buy bet." No matter how you juggle the buy bets, however, you still face a higher house edge than if you make pass and come bets or make place bets on the 6 or 8.

THE LAY BET

The **lay bet** is the opposite of a buy bet and is used by don't bettors. As with the buy bet, there is a 5% commission, except that the 5% is figured on the potential win rather than the amount of the wager. For instance, a $40 bet on the 4 would be charged a $1 commission because if the bet won, the payoff would be $20. As shown in the chart below, a 4 is paid off at 1:2 odds.

ODDS PAID FOR EACH LAY NUMBER			
Number	Ways to Roll	Odds Paid	House Edge
4	3	1 to 2	2.4%
5	4	2 to 3	3.2%
6	5	5 to 6	4.0%
8	5	5 to 6	4.0%
9	4	2 to 3	3.2%
10	3	1 to 2	2.4%

THE PLACE NUMBER WAGERS

Like all don't bets, the payoff for a lay bet is always less than the amount of the bet. This is because a 7 can be rolled six ways, which is more than for any other number. Since the chance of winning is better than even, a fair payoff would have to be less than even.

As the chart shows, the house edge for lay bets is always more than for buy bets. Making bets in odd amounts, however, can drive the house edge higher because most casinos round the commission up to the next dollar. To avoid paying excess commission, use a multiple of $40 for lay bets on the 4 or 10, a multiple of $30 on the 5 or 9, and a multiple of $24 on the 6 or 8.

If you find a casino that rounds down, you can reduce the house edge significantly by betting an amount that results in a win of just under $40. For example, a lay bet of $78 on the 4 or 10 will have a house edge of 1.3%, $57 on the 5 or 9 will have an edge of 1.7%, and $42 on the 6 or 8 will have an edge of 2.3%.

Unlike buy bets, which are always off during a come-out, lay bets are always working. Like buy bets, you can remove your lay bet at any time. Just be sure the dealer returns the commission along with the bet, if it was charged up front. Since the bet was not resolved, it was as though the bet was never placed.

Lay bets are not a good way to go for most craps players. They are mainly used by don't bettors who have already made don't pass and don't come bets, but aren't satisfied until they have covered the rest of the numbers. Even for don't bettors, this is not good craps strategy.

8

THE REMAINING BETS

The rest of the wagers on the craps layout are all described in this chapter. These are the bets that an astute craps player should never make, and are only covered here so the reader doesn't have to take my word for this. Saying they are bad bets is an understatement—with a house edge that ranges from 5.6% to 16.7%, they are better described as terrible bets. Between the various line wagers, come wagers, and place wagers covered in earlier chapters, there are plenty of bets for a craps player to choose from, so there is no need to ever make any of the following bets.

THE FIELD BET

As the name implies, a **field bet** covers a large group of numbers in a single bet. The numbers are 2, 3, 4, 9, 10, 11, and 12. This is a one-roll bet that one of these numbers will appear at the next roll of the dice. If one of the field numbers does appear, then you win even money except for the 2 or 12 which pay 2:1 odds. If one of the four missing numbers, 5, 6, 7, or 8, is rolled, then you lose the bet.

To make the bet, put your chips in the large box marked FIELD, which is just below the COME box. The FIELD box with its long string of numbers is prominent at both ends of the layout (see illustration) because the casino loves field bettors.

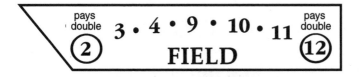

THE FIELD WAGER BOX

To a novice craps player, the field bet appears to be a good wager, since seven numbers can win and only four lose. This misinterpretation of the bet is what the casino banks on. Inexperienced craps players often make a field bet without first figuring their true chances of winning. Referring to the dice combinations chart in Chapter 4, if you add up the ways to make all the numbers in the field, the result is 16. Then add up the ways to roll the missing four numbers and you might be surprised to find that it is 20. Even paying double on the 2 and 12 doesn't make this a very good wager, with a house edge of 5.7%.

Casinos in downtown Las Vegas pay 3:1 instead of 2:1 on the 12. To meet the competition, more and more casinos on the Las Vegas Strip have also changed to a 3:1 payoff. This reduces the house edge to 2.8%. Even at these casinos, making a field bet is not the way to win at craps. It should be noted that on some field layouts there is a 5 in place of the 9, which makes no difference in the odds, since either number can be rolled four ways.

THE BIG 6 AND BIG 8 BETS

Near each end of the craps layout are two boxes marked BIG 6 and BIG 8, as shown in the illustration below. A wager on the big 6 (or 8) means you are betting that the shooter will roll a 6 (or 8) before rolling a 7. If you win, the bet pays even money.

BIG 6 AND BIG 8 BOXES

If you think that this wager looks exactly like a place bet on the 6 or 8, you are correct. There is just one significant difference: the house edge on the place bet is 1.5%, while the house edge on the big 6 or big 8 is a whopping 9.1%. This is because the place bet pays 7:6, while the big 6 or big 8 bet pays even odds for essentially the same bet. In fact, there are three ways to make a similar bet on the 6 or 8, as shown in the following chart.

POSSIBLE BETS ON 6 OR 8	
Wager	House Edge
Big 6 or 8	9.1%
Buy 6 or 8	4.7%
Place 6 or 8	1.5%

You would think that only greenhorn players, who know essentially nothing about craps, would ever wager on the big 6 or big 8 instead of making a place bet. Amazingly, this is not true, and the bet is not as unpopular as you might think. Although casinos should be ashamed to offer such a sucker bet, they can't help themselves when people keep throwing chips into the big 6 and big 8 boxes. Play it smart and don't go near those bets.

The only gambling jurisdiction where the big 6 and big 8 wagers are no longer offered is Atlantic City. Originally, the New Jersey Casino Control Commission required casinos to pay off big 6 and big 8 wagers at 7:6, which was the same as the place bet. Unlike place bets, which are fully controlled by the dealers, big 6 and big 8 bets are made directly by the players. At 7:6 odds, these bets became so popular that the dealers couldn't keep track of which bet belonged to which player, which resulted in many arguments. Since these disputes slowed down the game and reduced profits, the casinos requested the commission to eliminate the bet, which they eventually did.

More and more casinos in Las Vegas have also decided to do away with the big 6 and big 8 wagers. Hopefully, this is a trend that will spread to other jurisdictions.

THE PROPOSITION BETS

The proposition bets, **prop bets** for short, are mainly long-shot bets with high payoffs, which is why many players make them. Because the house edge ranges from a low of 9.1% to an astronomical 16.7%, prop bets are the worst bets on the craps layout. There is no reason to ever give the casino that kind of edge on a single wager.

The prop bets are all located in the center section of the layout (see illustration), and are controlled by the stickman. You simply toss him your chips and tell him which bet to put them on, and if you're a winner, he pays you. Since prop bets tend to invite math errors, to avoid being shorted, don't make a prop bet unless you know what it should pay.

There are two basic kinds of prop bets in the center section: the *hardway* bets and the *one-roll* bets. Except in Nevada, hardway bets are usually off during the come-out. In Nevada, you will hear the stickman call, "Hardways work unless you call them off on the come-out roll!" One-roll bets are working all of the time.

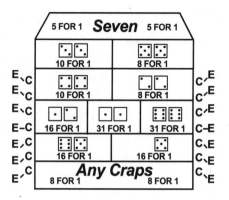

THE CENTER BETS

Hardway Wagers

When a point number comes up as a pair, it is referred to as the **hardway** because there is only one way it can be done. Since the sum of two identical numbers cannot be odd, the hardway has to be an even number, and there are just four such bets. A hardway 4 is when the dice show a 2+2, a hardway 6 is a 3+3, a hardway 8 is a 4+4, and a hardway 10 is a 5+5.

To win a hardway bet, the number has to be rolled as a pair before that number shows any other way or before a 7 appears. For instance, if you bet a hardway 6, you can only win if a 3+3 is rolled before a 5+1, 1+5, 4+2, 2+4, or a 7 (which can be made six ways). Because there are ten ways to lose this bet and there is only one way to win it, the odds against making it are 10 to 1. The casino, however, only pays 9 to 1 odds, which gives it an edge of 9.1%. The odds and the house edge for each of the four hardway wagers are shown in the following chart.

SUMMARY OF HARDWAY WAGERS					
Hardway Bet	Ways to Win	Ways to Lose	True Odds	Payoff Odds	House Edge
2+2	1	8	8 to 1	7 to 1	11.1%
3+3	1	10	10 to 1	9 to 1	9.1%
4+4	1	10	10 to 1	9 to 1	9.1%
5+5	1	8	8 to 1	7 to 1	11.1%

Don't be fooled by the fact that most craps layouts show the payoff odds for 2+2 or 5+5 as 8 for 1, and the payoff odds for 3+3 or 4+4 as 10 for 1. This is a common deception used by casinos to make you think the payoff is better than it really is (see Chapter 4).

ONE-ROLL WAGERS

The remaining proposition bets are called one-roll wagers because you either win or lose the bet on the very next roll of the dice. All one-roll wagers are bad bets with a house edge of 11.1% or higher. There is no reason to ever make these bets.

Any Seven
This wager is won if the next roll is a 7, and lost if any other number appears. Since there are six ways to make a 7, there are six ways to win and thirty ways to lose. Thus, the odds against winning are 5 to 1. The casino, however, only pays a winner 4 to 1 odds, which makes it the worst bet on the layout with a house edge of 16.7%

Any Craps
This wager is won if the next roll is a 2, 3, or 12, and is lost for any other number. There is one way to make a 2, one way to make a 12, and two ways to make a 3. Since there are four ways to win and 32 ways to lose, the odds against winning

are 8 to 1. The casino, however, pays only 7 to 1, giving it an edge of 11.1%.

The 2, 3, 11, and 12

Each of these one-roll wagers is in the lower half of the center section. A 2 or a 12 can be made one way each, which means the odds against either one are 35 to 1. When the payoff is 30 to 1, the house edge is 13.9%. A few greedy casinos, however, only pay 29 to 1 (30 for 1 on the layout), which kicks the house edge up to 16.7%.

Since a 3 or an 11 can be made two ways each, the odds against winning either of these bets is 17 to 1. When paid off at 15 to 1, the house edge is 11.1%. Those same greedy casinos, however, only pay 14 to 1 (15 for 1 on the layout) for a house edge of 16.7%.

Horn Bet

This is an ingenious wager thought up by the casinos that lets you make four sucker bets in one stroke. It is a simultaneous one-roll bet on the 2, 3, 11, and 12, and you have to toss out a multiple of four chips as though you made these bets individually. If you are fortunate enough to hit one of the numbers, you get paid accordingly, but the casino keeps the other three losing bets. Most of the time, the casino gets to keep all four of your bets. The house edge for the less greedy casinos is 12.5%. A variation of the horn bet is called the *horn high* bet, in which you double your bet on one of the numbers, so that you can lose even more.

Hop Bet

This bet is as ridiculous as the horn bet. Here you bet that a particular dice combination will come up on the next roll. For instance, you might wager that a 9 is rolled with a 3+6 showing on the dice. To do this, you tell the stickman that you want to bet the 3-6 on the hop. Since there are two ways to win (3+6 and 6+3), the odds against winning are 17 to 1. The casino, however, pays 15 to 1 for an edge of 11.1%.

A **hardway hop** bet is when your two chosen numbers are identical, such as a 3+3. Then there is only one way to win, and the odds against winning are 35 to 1. The casino pays this off at 30 to 1 for an edge of 13.9%.

Craps-Eleven

Known as a C&E wager, this is actually a combination of two separate wagers. The C portion is the same as the Any Craps bet, and the E portion is the same as a one-roll bet on 11, as described above. The payoffs are the same as for the individual bets. When you make this bet, the stickman puts your chips on the C and E circles at either side of the center section, in case you wonder what they are for.

9

SUMMARY OF ALL CRAPS WAGERS

LINE & COME/ DON'T COME WAGERS		
WAGER	**PAYS**	**HOUSE EDGE**
Pass or come	Even money (1:1)	1.41%
with 1x odds	1:1 plus true odds	0.85%
with 2x odds	1:1 plus true odds	0.61%
full double odds	1:1 plus true odds	0.57%
with 3x odds	1:1 plus true odds	0.47%
with 3-4-5x odds	1:1 plus true odds	0.37%
with 5x odds	1:1 plus true odds	0.33%
with 10x odds	1:1 plus true odds	0.18%
with 100x odds	1:1 plus true odds	0.021%
Don't pass or don't come	Even money (1:1)	1.36%
with 1x odds	1:1 plus true odds	0.68%
with 2x odds	1:1 plus true odds	0.45%
with 3x odds	1:1 plus true odds	0.34%
with 5x odds	1:1 plus true odds	0.23%
with 10x odds	1:1 plus true odds	0.12%
Note: The odds portion of a come bet is turned OFF during a come-out; all other bets remain ON.		

SUMMARY OF ALL CRAPS WAGERS

MULTI-ROLL WAGERS			
WAGER	**DESCRIPTION**	**PAYS**	**HOUSE EDGE**
Place 4	4 before 7	9:5	6.67%
Place 5	5 before 7	7:5	4.00%
Place 6	6 before 7	7:6	1.52%
Place 8	8 before 7	7:6	1.52%
Place 9	9 before 7	7:5	4.00%
Place 10	10 before 7	9:5	6.67%
Buy 4	4 before 7	39:20	1.67%
Buy 5	5 before 7	29:20	2.00%
Buy 6	6 before 7	23:20	2.27%
Buy 8	8 before 7	23:20	2.27%
Buy 9	9 before 7	29:20	2.00%
Buy 10	10 before 7	39:20	1.67%
Lay 4	7 before 4	19:41	2.44%
Lay 5	7 before 5	19:31	3.23%
Lay 6	7 before 6	19:25	4.00%
Lay 8	7 before 8	19:25	4.00%
Lay 9	7 before 9	19:31	3.23%
Lay 10	7 before 10	19:41	2.44%
Big 6	6 before 7	1:1	9.09%
Big 8	8 before 7	1:1	9.09%
Hardways 2+2	Hard 4 before 7 or easy 4	7:1	11.11%
3+3	Hard 6 before 7 or easy 6	9:1	9.09%
4+4	Hard 8 before 7 or easy 8	9:1	9.09%
5+5	Hard 10 before 7 or easy 10	7:1	11.11%

Note: All the above bets are turned OFF during a come-out, except the Lay bets, which are always working. In Nevada, the hardway bets are usually working.

BEAT THE CRAPS TABLE

ONE-ROLL WAGERS			
WAGER	**DESCRIPTION**	**PAYS**	**HOUSE EDGE**
Field bet - loose	2,3,4,9,10,11,12 on next roll	Even or 2:1, 3:1	2.78%
Field bet - tight	2,3,4,9,10,11,12 on next roll	Even or 2:1	5.56%
Any seven	7 on next roll	4:1	16.67%
Any craps	2,3, or 12 on next roll	7:1	11.11%
Bet on 2	2 on next roll	30:1	13.89%
Bet on 3	3 on next roll	15:1	11.11%
Bet on 11	11 on next roll	15:1	11.11%
Bet on 12	12 on next roll	30:1	13.89%
Horn bet	2,3,11, or 12 on next roll	27:4 on 2 & 12 3:1 on 3 & 11	12.50%
Hop bet	Any 2 chosen numbers on next roll	15:1	11.11%
Hardway hop	Any chosen pair on next roll	30:1	13.89%
Craps-eleven	Combination of any craps bet and bet on 11	See above	11.11%
Note: All the above one-roll bets are ON during a come-out.			

80

10

MONEY MANAGEMENT

After you have won a sum of money as the result of diligent and intelligent play, you should reap the rewards that those winnings can provide. Too many gamblers win a pile just to fritter it away by losing it back to the casino or giving it to the IRS. The purpose of money management is to retain as much of that money as possible. Hopefully, the advice in this chapter will help you to evade those money traps.

CONTROLLING YOUR BANKROLL

Before you step up to any craps table, be sure you have designated a specific sum of money to risk for your playing session. Otherwise, you may end up like some impromptu gamblers who, after sustaining a losing streak, continue to dig for more money in an attempt to recoup their losses. By doing this, they may eventually lose their entire bankroll during the first day of a gambling trip, and then wonder what to do the rest of the time. Some will head for the nearest ATM and start using money that was never intended for gambling. That is bad news, and is a trap that you don't want to fall into.

To avoid such a situation, let's say you are on a two-day gambling junket and have allocated $2000 that you can afford to lose. Divide that bankroll into two $1000 stakes, one stake for each day. Whatever you do, don't gamble away more than $1000 in any one day, and stay away from the ATMs. You must be disciplined about this.

BEAT THE CRAPS TABLE

IMPORTANT NOTE: *If you can't maintain that kind of money discipline, you have a problem and should seek out help. Although they would rather not, most casinos will tell you where to go or who to call to get the necessary help. If you don't do this, you can ruin your life.*

If your discipline is marginal, bring only the designated $1000 with you into the casino. Leave the rest of it with your wife or lock it up in the room safe. If you lose the entire $1000 stake, quit gambling for the day. Go sightseeing, see a show, have dinner, but don't gamble another cent until the following day.

The next day, repeat the procedure with the second $1000, but try not to lose it all this time. If you did lose your daily stake on the first day, you should carefully read the upcoming section, "When to Quit." By dividing your allocated gambling funds into daily stakes, you are maintaining a measure of control over your bankroll. Even if you do eventually lose it all, this form of monetary discipline will assure that you can do some gambling every day, which is the reason you went on the trip in the first place.

Now that you have determined your daily bankroll allocation, you should break that stake down for your individual gambling sessions. If you have decided that you will probably hit the tables twice a day, divide that $1000 daily allocation in half and don't step up to a table with more than $500 in your pocket. If you lose that amount and don't dig for more, you will be assured of having another playing session that day—and this time you may come out ahead.

PERSONAL BETTING LIMITS

You should determine ahead of time how much you can afford to bet. Craps is a rather volatile game, which means you may lose on several rolls of the dice before you start winning (or vice versa). If you want to stay alive for any length of time, you should not step up to a $25 minimum table with only $200 in your pocket. After making pass and come wagers with odds, a seven-out will break you very quickly. How much, then, do you need to weather the ups and downs?

That depends on your betting style. If you are using the conservative strategies in this book, you should have a gambling bankroll of at least forty times your basic wager for every playing session. This is based on the fact that you would be betting on no more than two points, and unless you are winning steadily, you would only be taking single odds. Assuming a one-unit basic wager, your total risk is not likely to exceed five units. Thus, the 40x rule would allow for eight straight losses, which is highly unlikely if you play sensibly by following the advice in this book.

Applying the same reasoning as above, if your playing style is more aggressive, your bankroll should be sixty to 100 times your basic wager. This is based on betting three or four points, which would require six to ten units per betting cycle.

Let's say you use a conservative strategy and have allocated $400 for a gambling session. The recommended basic wager would be no more than $10 ($400 ÷ 40 = $10). Thus, with a $400 bankroll, you shouldn't place an initial bet of more than $10 on each of two points. If, during your first playing session, you come out ahead, you can then readjust your betting level.

WHEN TO QUIT

The gambler who doesn't know when to quit will never come out ahead, no matter how well he plays. A commonly-heard piece of advice is: "Quit while you are ahead." That's good advice, except that many people misinterpret it to mean: "Quit while you are winning." No, no, no! The correct rule is:

NEVER QUIT WHILE YOU ARE WINNING!

When you get on a hot winning streak, you should always stick with it and slowly increase your bet size. Of course, you never know in advance when the streak will end, but sooner or later it will. When you do start losing, cut the size of your bets right down to the minimum, and if you continue to lose, quit playing. In other words:

QUIT ONLY WHEN YOU ARE LOSING!

But what if you win a few and lose a few, and the house is slowly grinding down your bankroll? Once you realize what is happening, take a break or at least change tables before you lose your entire daily stake. If you maintain the proper discipline, whenever you have gone through your daily gambling allotment, you are through gambling for the day.

Whatever you do, never try to recoup losses by increasing your bet size. Risking more money will not change your luck or change the inherent odds of the game you are playing. If you are on a losing streak, bigger bets will only cause you to lose faster.

You need to recognize those specific situations when your best option is to quit playing. Although there are some situations that you will have to determine for yourself, the following list covers most of them:

• When you are losing.

MONEY MANAGEMENT

- When you try to recoup by increasing your bet size.
- When you try to recoup by making long-shot bets.
- When you are unhappy with one or more dealers.
- When you are unhappy with one or more players.
- When you are angry, for whatever reason.
- When you are depressed.
- When you are not feeling well.
- When you are tired.
- When you have sucked down too many free drinks.

If you are on a winning streak, however, grit your teeth and stick with it, even if you are unhappy, angry, or tired. Remember: *Never quit while you are winning!*

MONEY MANAGEMENT REMINDERS

- Never play with money that you can't afford to lose—your chances of losing are greater than your chances of winning.

- Never step up to a craps table without first having designated specific funds for your gambling session.

- Never change your pre-established bankroll rules and dig for more money if you lose your allocated stake for the session or for the day. Instead, quit playing.

- Never deviate from smart playing strategy. And you should know what that is.

- Never try to chase your losses.

DEALING WITH THE IRS

The relationship between gambling and the IRS is a complex subject that even confounds lawyers and accountants specializing in taxes. In this section, I am not giving you any specific tax or legal advice, but only making you aware of certain IRS requirements. It is valuable to know about some of these things before encountering them in a real situation.

If you engage in casino transactions of more than $10,000, you should consult an accountant familiar with gaming laws. Casinos must report all cash transactions in excess of $10,000 to the IRS. They must also report an aggregate of cash transactions that occur within a twenty-four hour period and total more than $10,000. If you place a large bet at a sports book, cash-in chips, or even cash a check larger than $10,000, it must be reported. This is just a reporting requirement (presumably to control money laundering) and doesn't mean you have to pay taxes on the transaction. The state of Nevada also has a similar reporting requirement.

The IRS rule that is most important to gamblers is the requirement for the casino to report any lump sum win of $1200 or more by submitting a W-2G form. This, of course, refers mainly to slot machine jackpots, keno payouts, bingo prizes, and the like. Ordinary craps players don't have to worry about this requirement.

If you won a lump sum during a craps tournament, however, the IRS reporting requirement drops to $600. For this kind of a win, the casino has to submit a 1099-MISC form.

You would have to be a heavy craps better to win $1200 in one roll. And you might lose it all on the next hand or the next roll of the dice. The casino is not required to keep track of a craps player's wins and losses, but if you are a big bettor, it would be prudent to keep your own record. In any case, the casino is not required to withhold taxes unless the net winnings exceed $5000 or a payoff is at least 300 times the amount of the wager—which can't happen in craps.

Gambling winnings are considered ordinary income by the IRS and must be reported under "Other Income" on your 1040 tax return. If you are unfortunate enough to have a casino report your winnings, be sure you attach a copy of the W-2G or 1099-MISC to your return, or you will eventually get a letter from the IRS asking where it is.

If you are saddled with reported wins, you can reduce the tax burden (up to the amount of your winnings) if you can prove that you had offsetting gambling losses in the same year. Such losses cannot be subtracted from itemized winnings, but must be listed separately on Schedule A under "Miscellaneous Deductions." However, if your itemized deductions don't exceed the standard deduction, your gambling losses will not be useful as an offset. Also, keep in mind that you cannot reduce your overall tax by taking a net gambling loss—you can only offset winnings.

How do you prove that you had gambling losses? By keeping a detailed diary of all your gambling activities. How detailed? The IRS recommendation is that you record the date, the time, the amount of your wins and losses, and the type of game. You should also record the name and location of the casino, and the names of any people (witnesses) with you at the time. Supporting documentation such as airline ticket receipts and hotel bills will help to convince an IRS auditor that you were actually there. However, unless you are a professional in the business of gambling and your trip was primarily for business purposes, do not try to deduct expenses such as transportation, hotel rooms, or restaurants.

Once you get used to the idea, you will see that keeping a

diary is not as daunting as it first appears. How you actually deal with it, that is, what you put in and what you leave out, is entirely your decision. Just keep in mind that if the entire diary does not appear to be reasonable, an auditor may judge that it is inaccurate and disallow it.

11

THE FUNDAMENTALS OF CRAPS BETTING STRATEGY

Since craps is a negative expectation game, there is no betting strategy that will guarantee winning over the long-term. There are intelligent strategies, however, that can minimize losses and take advantage of winning streaks. This chapter, and those that follow, describe the strategies used by the most accomplished craps players, many of whom are consistent winners.

GENERAL BETTING ADVICE

Although there are more than forty different wagers available at a casino craps table, the strategies described in this book utilize only the following five or six bets.

- Pass line wager with odds
- Come wager with odds
- Place bet on 6 or 8
- Don't pass wager with odds
- Don't come wager with odds

The bets listed above are the only ones a craps player should normally make. The other bets on the craps layout are hardly ever recommended. Of course, if you have an intuition and feel lucky, you are free to throw your money away, but don't say I didn't warn you.

With one exception, the casino will allow you to make any craps wager at any time. The single exception is the don't pass bet, which may only be made before a come-out roll, that is, before a point is established. Because you are allowed to make all other bets whenever you want to, it doesn't mean you should. The wagers we do recommend, therefore, should only be made at appropriate times, as described in the strategies.

A common example of a badly-timed wager is placing a chip on the pass line after a point has already been established. This is usually done by a person who just stepped up to the table, saw that the point was a number he liked, and decided to bet on it. This is a legal, but dumb bet.

Why is it dumb? Because if the person won his pass line bet, the payoff would be even money, regardless of the number. That is, if he bet $10, on a point of 9, he would win $10. If, instead, he put his $10 on a place bet of the same number, his winnings would have been $14. Suppose he wasn't quite so dumb and took double odds on the pass bet? He would then win $40 ($10 + ($20 x 3/2)) for his $30 investment. The same $30 on a place bet of the same number would have paid $42 ($30 x 7/5), so he would have still been better off with the place bet. If this doesn't make mathematical sense, you should reread Chapters 4, 5, and 7.

QUALIFYING THE SHOOTER

Quite often, in an ongoing craps game, the dice seem to favor the shooter and he can do no wrong. At other times, the dice seem to consistently go against the shooter. In other words, the game can be streaky—where everyone is winning for a while and then everyone is losing for a while.

When many pass bettors first step up to a craps table, they don't want to risk betting into a losing streak. To avoid this, they wait for an eligible shooter before making their first bet. They define an eligible shooter as one who has thrown a 7 on the come-out or has made at least one point, and that's when they make their first wager.

Another qualification strategy is to wait for a shooter, after a point is established, to make at least five rolls without sevening out. The count can begin at any time, just so long as a point has been established. Thus, you can step up to a table in the middle of a round and begin counting the rolls.

There are many other shooter qualification schemes, and some of them get quite complicated, but they are not necessarily any more effective than the two simple ones described above. Once you have become an experienced craps player, you can invent rules to suit yourself. Whatever you do, the idea is to avoid betting into a cold shooter right off the bat.

The argument against qualifying a shooter is that craps is a completely random game, so it doesn't make any difference when you start betting. That is, a seemingly hot shooter may crap out on the next come-out, or seven-out on the next point.

This may be true, but some shooters seem to be able to hold on to the dice much longer than others, and they help everyone at the table to win. A cold shooter, of course, could turn hot, but will probably lose the dice before that happens. What we're saying is that it might not help much, but it surely doesn't hurt to wait for an eligible shooter. If you agree with the eligible shooter theory, then you should also wait for a new shooter to establish eligibility every time the dice pass.

In a later chapter, I will explain how to spot a shooter who sets the dice and has some control over the outcome of each roll. If you encounter such an occasion, it is a win-win situation for everyone who knows how to take advantage of it.

AN ELEMENTARY STRATEGY

Many beginning craps players make serious betting mistakes, and then become disgusted with the game because they keep losing money. Often, they will bet the field or the big 6 and big 8. Many are lured by the seemingly high payback odds of the proposition bets, and then wonder why they seldom pay off.

New craps players should start by only placing simple pass-line bets that have the greatest chance of winning. Once they have become comfortable with the game and have acquired a good working knowledge of the various wagers, they can graduate to more complex betting schemes. Until then, however, it is important that they stick with a good elementary strategy, such as the one described in this section.

The most basic wager on the craps table is the pass-line bet, and it is also the best bet for a novice to make—especially if the extra odds are taken. To do this properly, first determine the appropriate size of your bet from the guidelines in the chapter on Money Management, and bet this amount on the pass line just before the next come-out (when the black side of the puck is up). If the shooter passes or craps on the come-out, you should repeat the bet regardless of whether you won or lost. Continue repeating the bet so long as the shooter keeps passing or rolling craps.

Sooner or later the shooter will roll a point. When this happens, put an odds bet next to your original bet. Remember that if the point is 6 or 8, the odds bet should be a multiple of five, and if the point is 5 or 9, it should be an even number of dollars. In this elementary strategy, we are taking single odds, so the odds bet should be an amount as close to the original bet as possible. Taking the odds is important because it reduces the house edge to well under 1%.

Continue betting in this way until it feels natural to you.

THE FUNDAMENTALS OF CRAPS BETTING

Whatever you do, don't listen to the stickman and make any of the high-odds bets that he might suggest. If the shooter is hot and you have won an amount at least twice your original wager (pass plus odds), start taking double odds.

Anytime you begin losing, go back to taking only single odds. If you lose twice in a row you may want to quit betting until you qualify a new shooter. If you lose twice in a row with the new shooter, quit betting and leave the table.

Keep using the same strategy until you are very comfortable with it. The Elementary Strategy may seem simplistic and boring, but it gives you as good of a chance at winning as any other bets on the table, so you should stick with it until you feel reasonably competent. Then you can safely advance to the Conservative Strategy in the next chapter.

EXAMPLE OF ELEMENTARY STRATEGY

Action: Make a $15 pass-line wager just before the next come-out roll.

Come-out roll is a 3. This is craps, so the hand is over and all pass bets lose. You lose $15.

Action: Make another $15 pass-line wager.

Come-out roll is a 9. A point of 9 is established.

Action: Take $16 odds on your pass bet. (Because the point is 9, your single odds bet should be an even number.)

First point phase roll is a 5. The pass bets are unaffected.

Second point roll is a 3. Although this is craps, the pass bets are unaffected.

Third point roll is a 9. The shooter made his point, the hand is over, and the pass bets win. You win $15 on your pass bet plus $24 on the odds portion (which paid 3 to 2), for a total of $39. Your net gain is now

$39 - $15 = $24.

Action: Make a $15 pass-line wager.

Come-out roll is a 7. This is a pass, so the hand is over and all pass bets win. You win $15 on your pass bet and your net gain is $39.

Action: Make another $15 pass-line wager.

Come-out roll is a 4. A point of 4 is established.

Action: Take single odds of $15 on your pass bet.

First point roll is a 10. The pass bets are unaffected.

Second point roll is a 4. The shooter made his point, the hand is over, and the pass bets win. You win $15 on your pass bet plus $30 on the odds portion (which paid 2 to 1), for a total of $45. Your net gain is $84.

Action: Make a $15 pass-line wager.

Come-out roll is a 6. A point of 6 is established.

Action: You are $84 ahead, so you take double odds of $30 on your pass bet.

First point roll is a 7. This is a seven-out, so all pass bets lose and the shooter loses possession of the dice. You lose $45 on your pass bet and odds.

Action: You are down to a net gain of $39. Continue making pass bets, but cut back to single odds. If the new shooter is also a loser, quit betting and leave the table. Had you continued to win, however, you would have incrementally increased your odds bet (1x at a time) whenever your net gain doubled, to as much as the craps table allowed.

COMMON STRATEGY ERRORS

If I keep making center bets, sooner or later I'll get a 30 to 1 payoff and win big.

Yes, you will get a big payoff, but most of the time you will have lost much more than you won. The 2 and the 12 may pay 30:1, but each of these numbers will appear an average of once in every thirty-six rolls. The payoff doesn't begin to compensate for the risk, which gives the house a 13.9% edge.

If I haven't seen a 7 in over ten rolls, wouldn't the 7 be due and wouldn't that be a good time to make a bet on Any Seven?

The dice don't have a brain and don't contain a memory chip, so there is no way they can know that a 7 hasn't appeared for a while. The long-term probability of a 7 being thrown is 6 times in thirty-six rolls, and this probability does not change from roll to roll. If the law of averages was absolute, a 7 would regularly appear once in every six rolls. The fact that this does not happen shows that the dice are random, and that each roll is an independent event, which has no bearing on what happened on previous rolls. Consequently, the Any Seven wager has the same chance of winning or losing no matter how often a 7 has appeared or not appeared.

But, doesn't the law of averages mean that sooner or later a 7 has to appear more often for the mathematical odds to be correct?

Not really, but even if that were true, the correction might not occur until next week or next year.

Isn't the Field Bet a good deal because you win on seven numbers and only lose on four?

At first glance, the field bet might appear to be a smart wager, but if you figure the dice combinations you'll change your mind. The 2 or 12 can be made one way, the 3 or 11 can be made two ways, the 4 or 10 can be made three ways, and the 9 can be made four ways. This adds up to 16 ways to win. The losing numbers are 5, 6, 7, and 8, which can be made four, five, six, and five ways, respectively, giving you 20 ways to lose. Even with a double payout on the 2 and a double or triple payout on the 12, this is still a poor bet.

If the come-out establishes a number I like,

shouldn't I make a pass bet at that time?

No. You would be much better off making a place bet on that number. If the shooter made his point, the payoff on the late pass bet would be even money, whereas the payoff on an equivalent place bet would be 9:5 on the 4 or 10, 7:5 on the 5 or 9, and 7:6 on the 6 or 8, all of which are better payoffs than even money.

If I'm losing, I like to increase my bets so that I can recoup faster when I start winning.

This is a very bad idea. Since there is no way to know ahead of time when your luck will turn, bigger bets will only cause you to lose faster. Risking more money will not change your luck or change the inherent odds of the game you are playing.

If, I double my wager every time I lose, won't I eventually recoup all my losses?

This is called a Martingale system and has been around for at least 300 years. It seems to work until you encounter a long losing streak. Then, in an attempt to retrieve your losses, you will run up against the table limit if you don't run out of money first. Even when starting as low as $5, a doubling system multiplies the amount of the bet really fast, i.e., $5, $10, $20, $40, $80, $160, $320, $640.

I don't like to memorize odds; why can't I just bet on certain numbers by intuition?

There are more bad bets than good bets on a craps layout. If you bet by intuition, you will end up making more bad bets than good ones, and you would be better off playing roulette.

12

BETTING WITH THE DICE

This book does not offer cute or novel craps strategies. There is no such thing as a guaranteed winning strategy, regardless of how much the purveyor of the information might charge. The strategies presented in this chapter are the tried and true betting routines that have been applied for a long time by the most astute and successful right bettors. As explained earlier, the term right bettor is used as a shortcut for describing players who bet with the dice. There is no implication of correctness. The next chapter covers strategies for betting against the dice.

CONSERVATIVE STRATEGY

Once a new player has gotten used to the game and no longer has trouble following the sequence of play, it is time for him to graduate from the Elementary Strategy described in the last chapter and start making additional wagers. The next best step is to follow the pass bet with a come bet, both with odds. This is a popular betting combination that is used by many conservative, but skillful and successful players.

As in the Elementary Strategy, you start by making a wager on the pass line just before a new come-out. If you think it helps, qualify the shooter (previous chapter) before you place your first bet. The size of your bet should be based on the guidelines in the chapter on Money Management. Once a point is established, you have to make two additional bets: (1) take single odds on your pass line bet and (2) make a come bet. The come bet should be for the same amount as your pass wager.

Now the shooter is in the point phase, and if he doesn't seven-out on the next roll (in which case, you lose your pass bet and win your come bet), you should take single odds on the come bet. You now have two bets working on two different points, each one with odds. If the shooter makes his point on that first point-phase roll, however, you win your pass bet and your come bet is still working. In that case, you should make a new pass-line wager. The idea is to always have a pass-line wager plus one come wager working at all times.

Until you are ahead, stay with the single odds wagers. If you begin to win steadily, to the point that your net gain is twice your total bet amount (pass bet with odds plus come bet with odds), start taking double odds. If you keep on winning, increase the odds incrementally to as much as the craps table allows.

Whenever you begin losing, however, go back to taking only single odds. *Never chase your losses!* Any time the shooter craps out, make another minimum pass-line wager. Sooner or later, when the shooter sevens-out, you may want to qualify the new shooter before you start betting again. Remember that there is no mathematical basis behind the concept of qualifying the shooter, however many gamblers like to go with streaks.

The Conservative Strategy is a fine betting system that is used by many smart and experienced players. If this strategy is comfortable for you, you should stick with it rather than advance to the more complex and riskier strategies that are described further on. Should you want to advance, be sure you have developed enough experience at the table that keeping track of your bets has almost become second nature.

EXAMPLE OF CONSERVATIVE STRATEGY

Action: Qualify the shooter (previous chapter) and then make a $15 pass-line wager.

Come-out roll is a 7. This is a pass, so the hand is over and all pass bets win. You win $15.

Action: Make another $15 pass-line wager.

Come-out roll is a 10. A point of 10 is established.

Action: (1) Take single odds of $15 on your pass bet and (2) make a $15 come wager.

First point phase roll is a 5. A point of 5 is established for the come bet. Your pass bet is unaffected.

Action: Take single odds of $16 on your come bet. (Because the point is 5, the odds bet should be an even number.)

Second point roll is a 3. Although this is craps, your pass and come bets are unaffected.

Third point roll is a 10. The shooter makes his point, the hand is over, and all pass bets win. You win $15 on your pass bet and $30 on your odds bet (which paid 2 to 1), for a total of $45. Your net gain is $60. Your come bet is unaffected and is still working.

Action: Make a new $15 pass-line wager

Come-out roll is a 7. This is a win for your pass bet and a seven-out for your come bet. The hand is over. You win $15 on your pass bet and lose $15 on your come bet. The odds portion of your come bet is returned to you because it was automatically turned off during the come-out. Since this roll was a wash, your net gain remains at $60.

Action: Make another $15 pass-line wager.

Come-out roll is a 4. A point of 4 is established.

Action: (1) Take single odds of $15 on your pass bet and (2) make a $15 come wager.

First point roll is a 10. A point of 10 is established for your come bet. Your pass bet is unaffected.

BEAT THE CRAPS TABLE

Action: Take single odds of $15 on your come bet.

Second point roll is a 10. The point is made for your come bet, and your pass bet is unaffected. You win $15 on your come bet plus $30 on the odds portion (which paid 2 to 1), for a total of $45. Your net gain is $105.

Action: Make a new $15 come bet.

Third point roll is a 7. This is a seven-out for the pass bet and a win for your come bet. The hand is ended and the shooter loses possession of the dice. You lose your $15 pass bet as well as the $15 odds portion, and you win your $15 come bet, for a net loss of $15. Your net gain dropped to $90.

Action: Qualify the new shooter and then make a $15 pass-line wager.

Come-out roll is an 8. A point of 8 is established.

Action: (1) Take single odds of $15 on your pass bet and (2) make a $15 come wager.

First point roll is a 6. A point of 6 is established for your come bet. Your pass bet is unaffected.

Action: Take single odds of $15 on your come bet.

Third point roll is an 8. The shooter makes his point, the hand is over, and all pass bets win. You win $15 on your pass bet plus $18 on the odds portion (which paid 6 to 5), for a total of $33. Your net gain is now $123. Your come bet is unaffected and is still working.

Action: Make a new $15 pass-line wager.

Come-out roll is a 9. A point of 9 is established.

Action: You are $123 ahead, so you take double odds of $30 on your pass bet.

First point roll is a 7. This is a seven-out for both your pass bet and your come bet. You lose your $15 pass bet as well as the $30 odds portion, and you lose your $15 come bet, along with the $15 odds portion. Your net gain dropped to $48.

Action: Qualify the new shooter and then make a $15

pass-line wager. Although you are still $48 ahead, you just lost so you cut back to single odds. If you start winning again, you may incrementally increase your odds bets (1x at a time) to as much as the craps table allows. In the event that you continue losing, however, you should quit betting on this shooter. If you lose twice on the next qualified shooter, stop betting and leave the table.

CONVENTIONAL STRATEGY

This is called a conventional strategy because it is the most common betting scheme used by knowledgeable craps players. It consists of a pass wager and two come wagers, so that there are as many as three points working at one time. This is a somewhat higher-risk betting system, but it pays off handsomely when a shooter makes a lot of sequential rolls without sevening out.

Two versions of the Conventional Strategy are presented below. Other than the amount of odds taken, both versions are essentially identical. The double odds version is a little riskier than the single odds version, but can also result in greater returns.

Single Odds Version

As before, you start by qualifying the shooter (if you wish) and then making a wager on the pass line just before a new come-out. Once the shooter establishes a point, you have to make two additional bets: (1) take single odds on your pass line bet and (2) make a come bet. The come bet should be for the same amount as your pass wager.

Now the shooter is in the point phase, and assuming he doesn't seven-out on the second roll, you should then take single odds on the come bet and make a second come bet. You now have two bets working on two different points, each one with odds, plus a new come bet for which a point has not yet been established. If, on the third roll, the shooter neither makes his point nor sevens out, take single odds on the second come bet. Assuming he didn't make his pass line point or your first come point, you now have all three of your bets working with odds.

This is the stage at which your wagers are at their greatest risk. If the fourth roll is a 7, all your bets are lost. However, by this time in the hand, there are many other possibilities that could have occurred. For example, he might have made his point at roll two, three, or four, in which case you would have made a new pass wager. He might also have made one of your come points, in which case you would have made a new come bet. The idea is to try to have a pass-line wager plus two come wagers working at all times.

As in the previous strategies, until you are sufficiently ahead in funds, stay with the single odds wagers. Once you begin winning steadily, start taking double odds. If you keep on winning, increase the odds incrementally to as much as the table allows. Anytime you begin losing, however, go back to taking only single odds. *Never chase your losses!*

The Conventional Strategy is the betting system used by most expert and successful players. You should not use this strategy until you have become experienced enough at the craps table that you can follow all of your wagers with absolutely no difficulty. In other words, tracking your three wagers and the odds on them should be second nature. If you even begin to lose track of what you are doing, you can lose much more than you gain. Should this ever happen, go back to the Conservative Strategy and make only one come bet at a time.

Double Odds Version
The betting sequence of the double odds version is the same

as for the single odds version. The only difference is that you start by taking double odds on the pass and come wagers. Then, if you are winning consistently, start taking triple odds, and whenever you start losing, go back to double odds.

EXAMPLE OF CONVENTIONAL STRATEGY (Single odds)

Action: Qualify the shooter and then make a $15 pass-line wager.

Come-out roll is a 10. A point of 10 is established.

Action: (1) Take single odds of $15 on your pass bet and (2) make a $15 come wager.

First point roll is a 5. A point of 5 is established for your first come bet. Your pass bet is unaffected.

Action: (1) Take single odds of $16 on your first come bet (on a point of 5, the odds bet should be an even number) and (2) make a second $15 come wager.

Second point roll is an 11. Your pass bet and come bets are unaffected.

Third point roll is a 10. The shooter makes his point, the hand is over, and all pass bets win. A point of 10 is established for your second come bet. You win $15 on your pass bet plus $30 on the odds portion (which paid 2 to 1), for a total of $45. Your first come bet is unaffected.

Action: (1) Take single odds of $15 on your second come bet and (2) make a new $15 pass-line wager.

Come-out roll is an 11. This is a pass and the hand is over. You win $15 on your pass bet. Your come bets are unaffected and are still working. You are $60 ahead.

Action: Make a new $15 pass-line wager.

Come-out roll is a 7. This is a win for your pass bet and a seven-out for both your come bets. The hand is over. You win $15 on your pass bet and lose $30 on your two come bets. The odds portions of your come bets are returned to you because they were automatically turned off during the come-out. You are now $45 ahead.

Action: Make another $15 pass-line wager.

Come-out roll is a 4. A point of 4 is established.

Action: (1) Take single odds of $15 on your pass bet and (2) make a $15 come wager.

First point roll is an 8. A point of 8 is established for your come bet. Your pass bet is unaffected.

Action: (1) Take single odds of $15 on your come bet and (2) make a second $15 come wager.

Second point roll is a 10. A point of 10 is established for your second come bet. Your pass bet and first come bet are unaffected.

Action: Take single odds of $15 on your second come bet.

Third point roll is an 8. The point is made for your first come bet. Your pass bet and second come bet are unaffected. You win $15 on your first come bet plus $18 on the odds portion (which paid 6 to 5), for a total of $38. You are $83 ahead.

Action: Make a new $15 come bet.

Fourth point roll is a 9. A point of 9 is established for your first come bet. Your pass bet and second come bet are unaffected.

Action: Take single odds of $15 on your first come bet.

Fifth point roll is a 10. The point is made for your second come bet. Your pass bet and first come bet are unaffected. You win $15 on your second come bet plus $30 on the odds portion (which paid 2 to 1), for a total of $45. You are $128 ahead.

Action: You make a new $15 come bet.

Sixth point roll is a 4. The shooter makes his point, the hand is over, and all pass bets win. A point of 4 is established for your second come bet. You win $15 on your pass bet plus $30 on the odds portion (which paid 2 to 1), for a total of $45. Your first come bet is unaffected and is still working.

Action: You are $173 ahead, so you take double odds of $30 on your second come wager and make a new $15 pass wager.

Come-out roll is a 7. This is a win for your pass bet and a seven-out for both your come bets. The hand is over. You win $15 on your pass bet and lose $30 on your two come bets. The odds portions of your come bets are returned to you because they were automatically turned off during the come-out. You are now $158 ahead.

Action: Although you are still ahead, you lost on the last roll, so you go back to single odds. If you lose again with this shooter, you should quit betting and wait for the next qualified shooter.

AGGRESSIVE STRATEGY

For those players who want to cover more than three points, the Aggressive Strategy extends the Conventional Strategy out to a fourth point. Since working more than two come bets at a time can sometimes result in a concentration of outside numbers (4, 5, 9, 10) that are harder to make, in the Aggressive Strategy the fourth point is covered by a single place bet on the 6 or the 8. You now have to keep track of four separate wagers, so this strategy should not be applied until you have accumulated considerable experience and feel very comfortable at the craps table.

Start the Aggressive Strategy by qualifying the shooter (if you wish) and then making a pass-line wager with double odds, followed on successive rolls by two come wagers, each with double odds, until three points are covered, exactly as previously explained in the Conventional Strategy. Then, assuming the dice are still hot, make a place bet on the 6 or

8. The amount of the bet should be similar to your pass wager plus odds, but should be a multiple of six (see sidebar). Select whichever of the two numbers is not already covered by your pass bet or your two come bets. If both the 6 and 8 are already covered, make a third come bet, instead. In this case, a third come bet is less risky, since the inside numbers are covered.

Some aggressive players like to parlay their pass-line wager whenever they win a pass bet on the come-out. This amounts to leaving the winnings in place and effectively doubling the pass bet. When a shooter is hot, this action can result in a nice return, but of course, the risk is higher.

FULL PAYOUTS ON PLACE BETS

Getting the correct payoff for a place bet was covered in the chapter on place bets, but is worth repeating here. A place bet on the 6 or 8 pays 7 to 6. To assure getting the full amount for a win, the place bet must be a multiple of $6. That is, a $12 wager will win $14, an $18 wager will win $21, etc. If you make the mistake of betting $10, for example, the correct payoff is $10 x 7/6, which is equal to $11.67. Most casinos don't deal in small change, so you will get paid only $11.

Try to keep four points working by replacing bets as they are won or lost. Maintain the ratio of one pass bet, two come bets, and one place bet. The place bet should always be your fourth bet and should never be made on any numbers other than the 6 or 8, or the house edge gets too high. Remember, the place bet and the odds on the come bets are turned off whenever there is a new come-out roll. Do not turn them on.

As in the other strategies, if things are going well and you are consistently winning most of your wagers, start taking triple odds on new bets. If the dice continue to perform well, keep increasing the odds incrementally (only on the new bets) to as much as the craps table allows. Sooner or later, however, the dice will turn cold. When this happens, immediately cut back to double odds, and if the dice continue to perform badly, stop betting and consider making some don't bets (see the next chapter).

If you need to look at an example to fully understand how the Aggressive Strategy works, then you don't have enough experience to use it. It is the strongest and riskiest strategy I care to recommend and should only be used by skilled players. If you decide to apply a betting scheme more aggressive than this one, you are on your own.

13

BETTING AGAINST THE DICE

Don't betting is not for beginners and is not for the timid. It is a useful technique for those experienced craps players who can read a table and who never chase their losses. Properly applied, it can be very profitable for the perceptive player.

As explained earlier, betting against the dice is almost the exact opposite of betting with the dice, and the house edge on line bets is comparable either way. You would think, therefore, that the best playing strategy is very similar for do and don't betting. It is, and it isn't.

It is similar in that you don't want to have too many points working at one time. It is different for two reasons, one good and one bad. The good reason is that you can't lose all your points in one roll. Although you can win all of your don't points on a seven-out, you can lose them only one at a time—as each particular point number is rolled.

The bad reason is that you cannot qualify a shooter ahead of time for don't bets. Of course, if you believe that qualifying the shooter doesn't help, there is no bad reason. Once a shooter has demonstrated that he is cold by sevening out, he has also lost possession of the dice, and by the time the dice get back around to him, he may have become hot. In other words, you have to take your chances on every new shooter. The best you can do is to make a don't-pass wager and defer further judgment on the shooter until after the come-out. If the shooter rolls a point, you should lay odds and continue betting; if the shooter craps out, you should make another don't-pass bet; and if the shooter throws a natural, you should back off and not make any more bets.

To begin with, you should try to find a cold table. As a general rule, hot tables are crowded and cold tables are not. A good approach is to play only in casinos with several craps tables and check out those with only a few players. However, for two good reasons, you should never step up to a table that has no players. First, such a table is an unknown quantity and, second, you will have to roll the dice, which you probably wouldn't want to do.

You shouldn't even think about don't betting unless you are at a cold table or one that just turned cold. If you see a crowded table clearing out fast, that is a sign that the table turned cold. Jump over there and take a look. And, unless you have a working crystal ball, do not try to anticipate when a hot table will turn cold—wait until it actually happens.

Once you have decided on a table, find a spot close to one of the inside dealers so that you can easily reach the don't come box on the layout. If you can't find a good playing position, the table is too crowded and you should re-evaluate your decision, since a crowded table is usually too hot for a don't player.

CONSERVATIVE DON'T STRATEGY

The first few times that you try don't betting, you need to stay with a conservative approach until you are very familiar with the don't betting process. In following this Conservative Strategy, you will make one don't pass wager and a single don't come wager, and try to maintain two points.

Do not start betting until a new shooter gets the dice and then make a don't pass wager before the come-out. The size of your bet should be based on the guidelines in the chapter on Money Management. Depending on the result of the come-out roll, you should take one of the following three actions:

1. If the shooter craps out, you won your line bet. Make another don't pass wager.

2. If the shooter throws a natural, you lost your line bet. Wait for the next shooter before making another don't pass bet.

3. If the shooter rolls a point, lay single odds on the don't pass wager and make a don't come bet for the same amount as the don't pass wager. Remember that when you lay odds, the amount you are allowed to bet depends on how much you may win, and that depends on the point (see sidebar). Thus, for a $10 don't pass bet, you have to adjust your single odds bet so that you can win no more than $10 on the odds portion of the bet.

LAYING THE CORRECT ODDS

The amount of odds that you can lay depends on the potential payoff. To lay 1x odds on a $10 pass bet, the amount should be whatever it takes to win $10, and to lay 2x odds the amount should be whatever it takes to win $20. When laying 1x odds, for instance, this amount would be $10 divided by the odds of winning, which depends on the point. Since the odds of winning on a point of 6 or 8 are 5:6, the amount to lay is $10 divided by 5/6, which equals $12. For a point of 5 or 9, the amount to lay is $10 divided by 2/3, which equals $15. For a point of 4 or 10, the amount is $10 divided by ½, which equals $20. For laying 2x odds on a $10 wager, these amounts are doubled.

The shooter is now in the point phase, and if he sevens-out on the next roll, you win your don't pass bet and lose your don't come bet. A new shooter will get the dice and you should start over by making a new don't pass wager.

If, instead, the shooter throws a valid point number, other than the established point, lay single odds on your don't come wager. The actual amount of the bet depends on the point, just as for the don't pass wager. You now have two bets working on two different points, each one with odds. If the shooter makes his point on that first point-phase roll, however, you lose your don't pass bet and your don't come bet is still working. In that case, you should make a new don't pass wager. The idea is to always have a don't pass wager plus one don't come wager working at all times.

Continue betting in this manner as long as the shooter does not hit another of your points. If he does, stop betting on this shooter. *Never chase your losses!* You should also stop betting on the shooter if he ever throws a natural on the come-out. If you stop betting for either of these reasons, start making minimum bets again when a new shooter gets the dice.

EXAMPLE OF CONSERVATIVE DON'T STRATEGY

Action: Wait for a new shooter and then make a $15 don't pass wager.

Come-out roll is a 2. This is craps, so the sequence is over and your don't pass bet wins. You win $15.

Action: Make another $15 don't pass wager.

Come-out roll is a 10. A point of 10 is established.

Action: (1) Lay single odds of $30 on your don't pass bet ($15 divided by ½ equals $30). (2) Make a $15 don't come wager.

First point roll is a 5. A point of 5 is established for your don't come bet. Your don't pass bet is unaffected.

Action: Lay single odds of $24 on your don't come bet. (With a point of 5, basing the odds calculation on $15 will result in a bet of $22.50. To make it come out in even dollars, base the calculation on $16, instead. Thus, $16 divided by 2/3 equals $24.)

Second point roll is a 3. Although this is craps, your don't pass and don't come bets are unaffected.

Third point roll is a 7. This is a seven-out, so the hand is over and the shooter loses possession of the dice. All your don't bets win. You win $15 plus $15 odds on your don't pass bet, and $15 plus $16 odds on your don't come bet, for a total win of $61.

Action: Make a $15 don't pass wager.

Come-out roll is a 6. A point of 6 is established.

Action: (1) Lay single odds of $18 on your don't pass bet ($15 divided by 5/6 equals $18). (2) Make a $15 don't come wager.

First point roll is a 4. A point of 4 is established for the don't come bet. Your don't pass bet is unaffected.

Action: Lay single odds of $30 on your don't come bet ($15 divided by ½ equals $30).

Second point roll is a 6. The shooter made his point, so the hand is over and you lost your don't pass bet. You lost $15 plus $18 odds, for a total loss of $33. Your don't come bet is unaffected. At this point, your net gain is $61 - $33 = $28.

Action: Make a $15 don't pass wager. If you lose a second point, stop betting on this shooter. Do not, however, take down your working bets.

CONVENTIONAL DON'T STRATEGY

This is the same as the Conservative Strategy except that you make a second don't come bet and try to maintain three different working points. Again, if the shooter hits two of your points or a natural on a come-out, stop making new bets on this shooter and wait for the next shooter. If you still have a bet or two working, take down the odds and let the bets run their course.

Two versions of the Conventional Don't Strategy are presented below. Other than the amount of odds taken, both versions are essentially identical. The double odds version is a little riskier than the single odds version, but can also result in greater returns.

Single Odds Version

When the next shooter is ready to start, make a don't pass bet, even if you still have a don't come bet working. If the shooter establishes a point, lay single odds on the don't pass bet and restore the odds to any come bet that may still be working. If the shooter doesn't seven-out on the next roll, make a second come bet. Then follow the previous rules regarding when to stop betting on this shooter.

The time to increase your bets is after a second seven-out, assuming you haven't lost more than one point in either hand. If a point is rolled at the start of the third hand, start laying double odds on all of your wagers. As long as the shooter doesn't hit two of your points or rolls a natural on a come-out, continue as before until you have two don't come wagers working with double odds.

By now you know that any time the shooter hits two of your points or throws a natural, you should stop betting. You should also cut back to single odds when you start betting on the next shooter. Whenever you lose on two shooters in a row, leave the table or, at least, stop betting on the don't side. *Never chase your losses!*

Double Odds Version

The betting sequence of the double odds version is the same as for the single odds version. The only difference is that you start by laying double odds on the don't pass and don't come wagers. Then, if you are winning consistently, start laying triple odds (if the casino allows triple odds), and whenever you start losing, go back to double odds.

AGGRESSIVE DON'T STRATEGY

Using this Aggressive Don't Strategy is not recommended for inexperienced craps players. It is strictly for the advanced player who can read the table, who doesn't fall into the trap of chasing losses, and who can easily keep track of his bets. Anyone who uses this strategy just to get more action, is likely to pay dearly for that action.

The Aggressive Don't Strategy simply consists of going to a third don't come wager. This may not seem very complicated, but having a fourth point working is considerably riskier and requires close attention concerning when to stop betting and when to take down odds. It is not a strategy for a player who can't give the game full concentration, such as someone who is not feeling well, who's mind is on other things, or who has been drinking.

Because of the risk level, laying more than single odds at the start of a betting sequence is not recommended. Of course, if the shooter sevens-out a couple of times, you should then begin increasing the odds on the don't pass and the don't come wagers.

Some aggressive players like to parlay their don't pass wager whenever the shooter craps out on the come-out. This amounts to leaving the winnings in place and effectively doubling the don't pass bet. When a shooter is really cold, this action can result in a nice return, but of course, the risk is higher.

As before, whenever the shooter hits two of your points or throws a natural, you should stop betting. You should also cut back to single odds when you start betting on the next shooter. Whenever you lose on two shooters in a row, leave the table or, at least, stop betting on the don't side. *Never chase your losses!*

14

DICE CONTROL

The ability of a shooter to control the outcome of a roll of dice at a standard casino craps table appears to be a controversial subject, but there is no question that more and more people are at least attempting this. No matter how carefully a casino tries to assure that every roll of the dice is completely random, there are always those individuals who have the will and the determination to overcome the casino controls.

The main attraction to dice control is that it is (at present) a perfectly legal way to beat the casino. As long as the dice are not switched and are thrown in a legal manner so that they bounce off the far wall of the craps table, the casino has no basis for a complaint. It is not easy to control the dice at a casino craps table, but there now seem to be a fair number of people who have acquired that ability. It is a talent that requires a steady, methodical approach and long periods of private practice.

The controversy actually centers on how accomplished these people are, and it is easy to understand why documentation is hard to come by and why the casinos would rather not discuss the subject. Although there is anecdotal evidence of individual achievements, the question is: how many people have become good enough to win the money? I think there are more winning dice controllers than is generally believed.

The reason I believe this is that it takes only an occasionally successful roll to overcome the house edge of 1.4%. In fact,

DICE CONTROL

it has been calculated that to overcome the house edge takes only one successful controlled roll out of 43. That is, one roll in which the dice should have sevened-out, but didn't.

The goal of most **control shooters** (also known as **rhythm rollers**) is to avoid rolling a 7, and it doesn't have to be done very often. As an example, assume a place bet on the number 8, for which the house edge is 1.52%. To drive this house edge all the way to zero, the shooter would have to eliminate only one 7 out of 36. If you think this is unbelievable, here are the calculations:

Start with the basic formula for figuring the house edge:

House Edge = (House Odds - Correct Odds)
    x (Probability of Winning)

For a place bet on 8, the house odds are 7/6 (7 to 6), which is the actual casino payoff on the wager. The correct odds are 6/5, which is based on six ways to get a 7 and five ways to get an 8. The probability of winning is 5/11, a figure that represents the ways to win (5) divided by the ways to win plus the ways to lose (5 plus 6). Put these numbers into the formula for the following result:

House Edge = (7/6 – 6/5) x (5/11) =
    (35/30 – 36/30) x (5/11) = -0.01515

Multiplying -0.01515 by 100 and rounding off gives the commonly stated house edge of -1.52% for a place bet on 6 or 8. The negative result indicates that it is a house edge; if it was positive, it would be a player edge.

Now for the example (the above calculation was only to show how the formula works): Theoretically, if a pair of dice are rolled *randomly* 216 times, a total of thirty-six 7s and a total of thirty 8s should appear. Assume a shooter, who is just learning to control the dice, is trying to avoid rolling a 7. The shooter, who is not very good yet, gets thirty-five 7s in 216 rolls, missing only one 7. Here's the calculation:

House Edge = $(7/6 - 35/30)$ x $(35/65)$ =
$(35/30 - 35/30)$ x $(35/65)$ = 0

It may be hard to believe that eliminating one 7 out of thirty-six reduces the house edge to zero, but the math proves it. Imagine how much the house will be losing when the shooter gets better and is able to eliminate three or four 7s in 216 rolls. If this doesn't convince you that successful dice control is possible, you might as well not waste your time reading the rest of this chapter.

Yes, all of the above is to convince you that dice control is very possible. The purpose of this chapter, however, is not to teach you how to control the dice, but to teach you how to recognize that another shooter at your table is doing it. Being able to spot a dice controller and taking advantage of the situation can be very profitable.

SETTING THE DICE

In order to toss the dice in a manner that would favor or disfavor certain numbers, the dice have to be held in a certain position. To accomplish that, the dice are **set** before they are picked up and tossed. This is done right after the dice are given to the shooter by the stickman.

An experienced dice controller will observe the position of the dice when they are sitting in front of the boxman so that he knows exactly how to rotate them when the stickman slides them over. In this way, he can set the dice within one or two seconds after receiving them, so that the action is hardly noticeable by the dealers and the players. The only reason this matters is that

DICE CONTROL

a shooter fiddling too long with the dice holds up the game and irritates everybody.

There are basically two ways to set the dice. The first, and most common, is designed to avoid rolling a 7, and is called a hardways set. The second way is designed to increase the probability of rolling a 7, and is called a seven set or a come-out set because it is only used on a come-out roll. Obviously, the come-out set is used by a shooter who makes only pass bets, so it is not employed as often as a hardways, and even then only for special situations.

A hardways set is easy to recognize because the pair of dice show a 2+2, 3+3, 4+4, or 5+5 on the top surface. Actually, it is a little more precise, in that the other three pairs should appear on the front, the back, and the bottom. When this is done, the 6 will be on the left side of both dice and the 1 will be on the right side, effectively isolating two of the 7s, as shown in the illustration.

Hardways Set
with 4+4 on Top

Hardways Set
with 5+5 on Top

HARDWAYS SET

A hardways set, when used with a proper grip and a proper throw, minimizes the chances of rolling a 7. It is, by far, the most common set used by expert dice controllers.

GRIPPING THE DICE

Before the dice are thrown, it is important to grip them correctly. Once the dice are set, they should be picked up and lightly held between the fingers so that they remain together in the same position that they were set. Most experts grip the dice with the thumb spanning the intersection of the two dice on one side and two or three fingers on the opposite side. If you see this kind of a careful grip, you are probably looking at a control shooter.

Gripping the dice properly takes practice and concentration, so it is best to remain quiet while the shooter picks up the dice and tosses them. If you are standing next to the shooter, be especially careful not to cause any interference or jostling.

THROWING THE DICE

A control shooter will toss the dice in a gentle arc so that they land together just beyond the curve in the pass line and lightly bounce against the wall. If there are chips in the way, the shooter will ask the players to move their chips over a little. Striking chips or any other obstruction destroys the controlled action of the dice. Most of the time, of course, hitting the wall also impairs the control, but much of the time the dice retain their relative positions well enough to get the job done.

Learning to grip and throw the dice properly takes long hours of practice on a real craps table or a mock-up that accurately simulates the action of a casino table. I don't expect you to actually learn to do this, but just to learn how it is done so that you recognize a control shooter when you see one.

SPOTTING A CONTROL SHOOTER

Here is the crux of this chapter: recognizing a control or rhythm shooter at a craps table. If you have read and absorbed the information in this chapter, it should be easy to do. The following is a summary of what to look for.

A control shooter...

- Stands next to or close to the stickman so as to minimize the throwing distance.
- Sets the dice before picking them up.
- Grips the dice carefully, without changing their relative positions.
- Asks that obstructions or chips in the landing area be moved to one side.
- Throws the dice smoothly and consistently so that they stay together, land near the flat portion of the wall, and strike the wall lightly.
- Appears to be completely focused on the task of shooting the dice.

A random shooter...

- Stands anywhere at the table, including the far end.
- Grabs the dice and shakes them.
- Throws the dice so that they skip down the table.
- Exhibits no form or consistency.
- Doesn't especially concentrate on the task of shooting the dice.

When your observations pay off and you finally spot a shooter who appears to be controlling the dice, watch the shooter's betting patterns and emulate them. A control shooter is unlikely to make wagers other than pass and come bets. Be careful about making come bets, since a shooter who makes only pass bets is probably trying to roll a 7 on the come-out and trying to avoid 7s after a point is established.

15

OTHER CRAPS GAMES

CRAPLESS CRAPS

Crapless Craps, also known as *Never Ever Craps*, is an old sucker version of casino craps that dates back to antiquity and is periodically revived. One of the more recent revivals was by Bob Stupak in the early 1980s when he offered the game at his Vegas World casino (now the Stratosphere). Then it lay dormant until the mid-1990s, when it reappeared in Mississippi.

The lure in Crapless Craps is that there are no craps numbers; there is no way to lose on the come-out. It seems like a good deal until you learn that the only way to win on the come-out is to roll a 7; the 11 is not a winner. In fact, if you roll an 11, it becomes the point. The former craps numbers of 2, 3, and 12 also become point numbers if they appear on the come-out.

Thus, all numbers except the 7 are potential points. This seems to be reasonable until you figure out that since there is only one way to roll a 2 or 12 and six ways to roll a losing 7, the odds of repeating those points are 1 in 7. Since there are two ways to get a 3 or 11, the odds of repeating those points are 1 in 4. In other words, if one of those former craps numbers becomes the point, you have an excellent chance of losing anyway. And, on top of that, the 11, which was an automatic win on the come-out, now could become a hard-to-make losing point.

ODDS OF REPEATING THE POINT BEFORE ROLLING A SEVEN IN CRAPLESS CRAPS

Point	Ways to Roll the Point	Ways to Roll a Seven	Odds
2 or 12	1	6	1 to 6
3 or 11	2	6	1 to 3
4 or 10	3	6	1 to 2
5 or 9	4	6	2 to 3
6 or 8	5	6	5 to 6

An odds bet is offered on all the point numbers, including the additional points of 2, 3, 11, and 12. On the 2 and 12, the odds are 6:1, and on the 3 and 11, the odds are 3:1. Crapless craps has a high house advantage, mainly caused by the loss of the 11 winner. The following chart shows a comparison of the house edge for crapless and traditional craps.

HOUSE EDGE FOR CRAPLESS AND TRADITIONAL CRAPS

Pass or Come Bet	Crapless	Traditional
With no odds	5.38%	1.41%
With 1x odds	2.94%	0.85%
With 2x odds	2.02%	0.61%
With 3x odds	1.54%	0.47%
With 5x odds	1.04%	0.33%
With 10x odds	0.58%	0.18%

It should be no surprise that the house percentage for crapless craps is almost four times higher than for the traditional game. Because of this heavy edge, there are no don't bets available on a crapless table. The don't bettor's advantage would be so strong that adjusting the don't payoffs downward to compensate would be impossible to do without it looking ridiculously obvious.

You can make a place bet on any number except the 7. As can be seen in the following chart, place betting the 6 or 8 is one of the best wagers in crapless craps. Of course, when you make place bets, you are not concerned with getting craps on the come-out, so you might as well be playing the traditional game.

CRAPLESS CRAPS PLACE BETS			
Place Number	True Odds	Payoff Odds	House Edge
2 or 12	6 to 1	11 to 2	7.1%
3 or 11	3 to 1	11 to 4	6.3%
4 or 10	2 to 1	9 to 5	6.7%
5 or 9	3 to 2	7 to 5	4.0%
6 or 8	6 to 5	7 to 6	1.5%

If you are really paranoid about losing to craps on the come-out, then, maybe crapless craps is the game for you. Just be aware that eliminating the losing craps numbers will end up costing you more in the long run.

PRIVATE CRAPS GAMES

Casino craps—where all bets, both for and against the dice, are covered by the house—is known as bank craps because the casino acts as a bank. In the private game, players bet against each other and there is no bank. Like so many other gambling games, craps was played as a private game long before it appeared in the casinos.

BEAT THE CRAPS TABLE

A private craps game is played in a very similar manner to the basic casino game. On the come-out, the 7 and 11 are winners for pass bettors, while the 2, 3, and 12 are losers. The reverse is true for the don't bettors. In the private game, the 12 is not a push, but is a winner for don't bettors. Consequently, the don't bettor has a 1.4% advantage over the pass bettor.

The remaining numbers (4, 5, 6, 8, 9, and 10) are points, which have to be repeated before a 7 shows for a pass bettor to win. After the come-out, players can lay or take odds on the point. An odds bet can be made whether or not a wager was placed on the come-out, and it can be made in any amount. For instance, if the point is 10, any player can lay 2:1 odds against the shooter or take 2:1 odds with the shooter.

In a game where all the players are experienced and know the odds, the wagers are almost always at the correct odds. When there are some unseasoned players, however, the odds offered are not always correct. Obviously, a complete knowledge of the odds is very important if you don't want to get taken by the sharpies.

In the private game, almost all wagers are line bets for or against the dice. If a point is established at the come-out, there is usually a round of odds betting on the point. There are no come bets or place bets because it is too difficult to keep track of them without a layout. Some players do make side bets on specific numbers; in fact, any kind of a bet can be made if the bettor can find a taker. Since there is no bank, the only criterion for any wager to be valid is that another player is willing to cover it.

A hand begins when a shooter throws down some cash and asks who will "fade me." He is showing how much he wants to wager and is asking who will cover the amount. One player may cover a portion of the bet and a second or third player may cover the rest. They do this by putting down enough money to match the shooter's cash. If the shooter's bet is covered, but there are more players who want to bet against (or with) the shooter, they throw out their money and say "Who'll fade me?" Any money that isn't faded is pulled back.

The players who cover the shooter's money are betting wrong because, in private craps, the shooter is always a pass bettor. A shooter who wants to bet wrong must give up the dice to the next shooter in the rotation.

Once all the initial bets are faded, the shooter rolls the dice. A 7 or 11 means the shooter wins and the wrong bettors who faded the shooter lose. A 2, 3, or 12 means the shooter loses and whoever faded the shooter wins. In private craps there are no barred numbers for wrong bettors. Except for the 1.4% advantage that this gives the wrong bettor, all bets are fair if everyone knows the correct odds.

Any other number thrown by the shooter becomes the point. Now the players may or may not make odds bets on the point number, and the shooter rolls again. The shooter continues to roll the dice until either the point is made, in which case the shooter wins, or a seven-out occurs, in which case the shooter loses. At that point the hand ends and the next roll is a new come-out.

The main problem with private craps is that it can be hard to tell if the game is honest. Someone produces a pair of dice and there is no way of knowing whether or not the dice are rigged. The dice are usually smaller than casino dice, have rounded edges, and may be badly worn.

To protect against misspotted dice, be sure that each of the three pairs of opposite faces add up to seven. Insist that when the dice are thrown, they always bounce against a vertical surface. Finally, know the other players and, most importantly, know the odds.

APPENDIX

This appendix contains the mathematical proof that the combined house edge percentages shown in this book for don't wagers with odds are correct.

HOUSE EDGE CALCULATIONS

The basic formula for figuring the house edge is...

House Edge = (House Odds - Correct Odds) x (Probability of Winning)

where the

$$\text{Probability of Winning} = \frac{(\text{Ways to Win})}{(\text{Ways to Win} + \text{Ways to Lose})}$$

To show how this formula works, we'll start with the simple case of a place bet on 8. To win this bet, an 8 has to be rolled before a 7 appears. The casino payoff on a win is 7/6 (7 to 6), which are the **house odds**. Since there are six ways to get a 7 and five ways to get an 8, the **correct odds** are 6/5. Finally, the **probability of winning** is 5/11 (five ways to win divided by the sum of five ways to win and six ways to lose). Put these numbers into the formula for the following result:

House Edge = (7/6 – 6/5) x (5/11)
= (35/30 – 36/30) x (5/11) = -0.01515

Multiplying -0.01515 by 100 and rounding off gives the

commonly-stated house edge of -1.52% for a place bet on 6 or 8. The negative result indicates that it is a house edge; if it was positive, it would be a player edge.

PASS-LINE BET

House edge calculations for line bets are more complicated because they consist of two parts: the come-out and the point phase. Furthermore, since it is not known ahead of time what point will be established, all the possible points have to be factored into the calculation. The best way to start is to figure the probability of winning.

There are six ways to get a 7 and two ways to get an 11, so the probability of winning on the come-out is: 6/36 + 2/36 = **8/36**.

The probability of establishing a point and then repeating it before a 7 appears is: (probability of a 4) times (probability of a 4 before a 7) plus (probability of a 5) times (probability of a 5 before a 7) plus (probability of a 6) times (probability of a 6 before a 7), etc. Putting in numbers for all six points, we get: (3/36)(3/9) + (4/36)(4/10) + (5/36)(5/11) + (5/36)(5/11) + (4/36)(4/10) + (3/36)(3/9) = **1206/4455**.

The overall probability of winning is 8/36 + 1206/4455 = **244/495**. Since there are 244 ways to win, there must be 495 – 244 = 251 ways to lose, and the correct odds are **251/244**. Since the casino payoff for a winning pass bet is 1 to 1, the house odds are **1/1**.

Putting these numbers into the formula, we get...

House Edge = (1/1 – 251/244) x (244/495) = -7/495 = -0.01414

Multiplying -0.01414 by 100 and rounding off gives the familiar house edge of -1.41% for a pass or come bet.

DON'T PASS BET

The house edge calculation for don't bets is essentially the same as for do bets except, of course, that some of the numbers are different because craps is a win on the come-out and a seven-out is a win after a point is established.

On the come-out, there are only two craps numbers, since the 12 is a push. There is one way of getting a 2 and two ways of getting a 3, so the probability of winning on the come-out is: 1/36 + 2/36 = **3/36**.

The probability of getting a 12 and pushing on the come-out is: **1/36**.

The probability of establishing a point and then getting a 7 before the point repeats is: (3/36)(6/9) + (4/36)(6/10) + (5/36)(6/11) + (5/36)(6/11) + (4/36)(6/10) + (3/36)(6/9) = **2352/5940**.

The overall **probability of winning** is: 3/36 + 2352/5940 = **2847/5940**. The probability of losing is 1 - (2847/5940 + 1/36) = 2928/5940, thus the **correct odds** are **2928/2847**. Since the casino payoff for a winning don't pass bet is 1 to 1, the **house odds** are **1/1**.

Putting these numbers into the formula, we get...

House Edge = (1/1 − 2928/2847) x (2847/5940) = -3/220 = -0.013636 = -1.36%

DON'T PASS BET WITH ODDS

Now we come to the reason for this appendix: the correct house edge calculation for a combined don't pass (or don't come) bet and laying odds. The best way to figure the combined edge is to divide the average gain by the average bet. The gain on the don't pass bet is -3/220 (see above) and the gain on the odds is zero. The actual amount of the odds bet depends on the odds multiple and the point. Assuming single odds and a basic don't pass bet of $10, a player can lay odds of $20 on the 4 or 10 for a win of $10, or $15 on the 5 or 9 for a win of $10, or $12 on the 6 or 8 for a win of $10.

The average gain is (10)(-3/220) = -30/220

The average bet is $10 + (2)[(3/36)($20) + (4/36)($15) + (5/36)($12)] = $10 + $10 = $20

The house edge for don't pass or don't come with single odds is (-30/220)/$20 = 0.006818 = 0.68%

For double odds, the average bet is $10 + (2)[(3/36)($40) + (4/36)($30) + (5/36)($24)] = $10 + $20 = $30

The house edge for don't pass or don't come with double odds is (-30/220)/$30 = 0.004545 = 0.45%

I believe that the above calculations are a correct way to arrive at the combined house edge for don't bets with odds.

GLOSSARY

Action: The total amount that you bet, regardless of wins or losses. If you bet $10 on fifty rounds, then your action was $500.

Any craps: A one-roll wager that the next number will be a 2, 3, or 12.

Any seven: A one-roll wager that the next number will be a 7.

Back line: See Don't line.

Bank: (a) Money on the table that is used by the dealer to pay winning bets. (b) The casino or the game operator. (c) Any person who covers all the bets in a game.

Bankroll: The total amount of money that a player has allotted to a gambling session.

Bar 12 (or 2): A rule that is printed on the layout in the don't pass and don't come areas. It means that during a come-out, the 12 (or the 2) is a push for don't bets.

Behind the line: An odds bet after a point is established.

Betting right: Betting with the dice; that a pass bet will win.

Betting wrong: Betting against the dice; that a don't pass bet will win.

Big 6: An even money bet that a 6 will be rolled before a 7.

Big 8: An even money bet that an 8 will be rolled before a 7.

Blacks: Black casino chips with a value of $100 each.

Bleeder: A paranoid casino supervisor who worries about players winning. Also called a sweater (one who perspires).

GLOSSARY

Boxcars: A slang term for a roll of 12.

Boxman: The supervisor of the craps table who sits between the two inside dealers.

Box numbers: The boxed numbers 4, 5, 6, 8, 9, and 10, which are used to mark the point, and to position the place, come, and buy bets.

Buy bet: A wager which is similar to a place bet, but is paid at correct odds, for which the casino charges a 5% commission.

Buy-in: (a) An exchange of a player's currency for casino chips. (b) The amount of money a player gives the dealer for the chips.

Cage: A shortened term for the cashier's cage.

Call bet: A verbal wager with no chips on the layout. Some casinos do not allow call bets.

Casino advantage: See House edge.

Center bet: See Proposition bet.

Check or cheque: Alternate term for Chip that is commonly used by casino personnel and professional gamblers.

Chip: A gaming token with an imprinted value that is used in place of real money at various table games in a casino. Chips may be redeemed for cash at the issuing casino. Also called house check, casino chip, or value chip. The terms Chip and Check are used interchangeably.

Cold hand, Cold dice: Dice that consistently don't pass, resulting in a losing streak for pass bettors and a winning streak for don't bettors.

Color change: A change in the denomination of chips.

Come bet: A bet with the dice made after the come-out roll.

Come-out roll: Any dice roll made before a point is

established.

Comp: A shortening for complementary. The term used for free meals, lodging, and other services provided by the casino to regular players.

Contract bet: A bet that has to remain in effect (can't be taken down or turned off) until it is resolved. Pass and come bets are contract wagers.

Correct odds: The true mathematical odds that a bet will win or that a point will be made. Also called true odds.

Crap-out: To throw one of the craps numbers on the come-out roll.

Craps: The name of the game. Also the term used for the numbers 2, 3, or 12.

Craps-eleven: A combination of an any craps bet and a one-roll bet on 11.

Crew: The casino employees who staff a craps table.

Dealer: Any of the casino employees at a craps table.

Dice: The two plastic cubes with one through six spots on the six sides, that are used to play craps.
Don't come bet: A bet against the dice that is made after the come-out roll.

Don't pass bet: A wager against the dice that is made prior to the come-out roll that the dice will not pass.

Don't pass line: The area on the layout where a don't pass bet is made.

Double odds: An odds wager made at double the amount of the original bet.

Easy way: A roll of a 4, 6, 8, or 10, where the numbers on the dice are not paired.

GLOSSARY

Edge: A statistical advantage. Usually the casino's advantage.

Even money: A wager that pays off at 1 to 1 odds, if it wins. That is, if a $10 bet wins, the original bet is returned along with an additional $10. Also called a flat bet or even odds.

Expectation: The average amount that may be won or lost in a particular game over an extended period of play. Also called expectation of winning.

Field bet: A one-roll wager that the next roll of the dice will be a 2, 3, 4, 9, 10, 11, or 12.

Flat bet: See Even money.

Floorman: A politically-incorrect term for floor supervisor.

Floor supervisor: A pit supervisor who reports to the pit boss. This is the person who watches dealers to assure that all losing bets are collected, winning bets are correctly paid, and nobody is cheating.
Front line: See Pass line.

Greens: Green casino chips with a value of $25 each. Also called quarters.

Hand: The series of dice rolls from one come-out to the next come-out. Also called a game, a round, or a shoot. Sometimes these terms are used to describe the entire time a shooter has possession of the dice.

Hardway: The numbers 4, 6, 8, or 10, when they come up as a pair, e.g., 2+2, 3+3, 4+4, or 5+5.

Hardway bet: A bet that 4, 6, 8, or 10 will be rolled as a hardway before the easy way appears or before a 7 appears.

Hop bet: A bet that a particular dice combination will come up on the next roll.

Horn bet: A simultaneous one-roll bet on the 2, 3, 11, and 12.

BEAT THE CRAPS TABLE

Hot hand, hot dice, hot roll: Dice that consistently pass, resulting in a winning streak for pass bettors and a losing streak for don't bettors.

House: The casino, the bank, or the game operator.

House edge: The difference between the actual odds and the payoff odds, usually stated as a percentage, which is the mathematical edge the house has over the player. Also called casino advantage, house percentage, or P.C.

House odds: The amount the house pays a winning bet, usually stated as an odds ratio such as 2 to 1. Also called odds paid or payoff odds.

Inside dealer: The craps dealer who stands next to the boxman and handles the bets at his end of the table. Sometimes called a standing dealer.

Inside numbers: The place bet numbers 5, 6, 8, and 9.

Lay bet: A wager which is the opposite of a place bet, made by a don't bettor and paid at correct odds, for which the casino charges a 5% commission.

Laying odds: An odds bet made by a don't bettor.

Layout: The imprinted surface of a gaming table displaying the various bets.

Limit: See Table limit.

Line bet: See pass bet.

Loaded dice: Crooked dice that have been weighted so that certain numbers are favored.

Marker: A casino IOU which permits a player to obtain chips against previously-established credit or money on deposit.

Maximum: See Table limit.

Minimum: The smallest bet allowed at a table.

GLOSSARY

Miss-out: See Seven-out.

Natural: A 7 or 11 rolled on the come-out resulting in a win for pass bettors. Craps dealers use the term to mean any number that results in the immediate resolution of the pass bets at the come-out (2, 3, 7, 11, or 12).

Nickels: See Reds.

Odds: The ratio of the number of ways to win versus the number of ways to lose.

Odds bet: A bet that is paid at the correct odds, which can be made on a pass, don't pass, come, or don't come bet after a point is established.

Odds paid: See House odds.

Off: A designation that a bet on the layout is temporarily not working.

On: A designation that a bet is working.

One-roll bet: A bet that is resolved by the next roll of the dice.

Outside numbers: The place bet numbers 4, 5, 9, and 10.

Pass: A winning decision for the dice: either a pass on the come-out or a made point.

Pass bet: A wager with the dice that is made prior to the come-out roll that the dice will pass. Also called a line bet or a pass line bet.

Pass line: The area on the layout where a pass bet is made. Also called the front line.

Payoff: The amount paid by the casino for a winning hand.

Payout: Same as payoff.

Payoff odds: See House odds.

BEAT THE CRAPS TABLE

P.C.: Gambler's abbreviation for percentage. See House edge.

Pit: The area behind a group of gaming tables that is restricted to casino employees.

Pit boss: The supervisor who is responsible for the tables in a specific pit or gaming area. The pit boss reports to the shift manager.

Place bet: A bet that a particular place number will be rolled before a seven. The place numbers are 4, 5, 6, 8, 9, and 10.

Point: If a 4, 5, 6, 8, 9, or 10 is rolled on the come-out, that number becomes the point.

Press: To increase a bet, usually by doubling it.

Proposition bet: Any of the wagers in the center of the craps layout. Also called a center bet.

Push: A tie between a player and the casino in which no money changes hands. Also called a standoff.

Quarters: See Greens.

Reds: Red casino chips with a value of $5 each. Also called nickels.

Right bettor: A player who bets that the dice will pass by making a pass or a come bet.

Roll: A throw of the dice.

Seven-out: The roll of a 7 after a point is established and before the point is repeated, causing pass bettors to lose and don't bettors to win. Also called a miss-out.

Shoot: See Hand.

Shooter: The player who is rolling the dice.

Silver: Casino chips or tokens with a value of $1 each.

GLOSSARY

Single odds: An odds wager made for the same amount as the original bet.

Snake eyes: A slang term for a roll of 2.

Standoff: See Push.

Stickman: The craps dealer who moves the dice around with a dice stick and controls the center bets.

Table limit: The largest bet allowed at a table, which may be increased for a high roller. Also called limit or maximum.

Taking odds: An odds bet made by a pass-line or come bettor.

Toke: Short for token, a gratuity given to the dealer.

True odds: See Correct odds.

Unit: The size of a basic bet that is used as a standard of measurement.

Working: A term indicating that a bet is currently active; is turned on.

Wrong bettor: A player who bets against the dice by making a don't pass or a don't come bet.

Yo, yo-leven: The stickman's verbal term for the number 11, to avoid confusion with the number 7.

GRI'S PROFESSIONAL VIDEO POKER STRATEGY
Win Money at Video Poker! With the Odds!

For the **first time,** and for **serious players only,** the GRI **Professional Video Poker** strategy is released so you too can play to win! **You read it right** - this strategy gives you the **mathematical advantage** over the casino and what's more, it's **easy to learn!**

PROFESSIONAL STRATEGY SHOWS YOU HOW TO WIN WITH THE ODDS - This **powerhouse strategy,** played for **big profits** by an **exclusive** circle of **professionals,** people who make their living at the machines, is now made available to you! You too can win - with the odds - and this **winning strategy** shows you how!

HOW TO PLAY FOR A PROFIT - You'll learn the **key factors** to play on a **pro level:** which machines will turn you a profit, break-even and win rates, hands per hour and average win per hour charts, time value, team play and more! You'll also learn big play strategy, alternate jackpot play, high and low jackpot play and key strategies to follow.

WINNING STRATEGIES FOR ALL MACHINES - This **comprehensive, advanced pro package** not only shows you how to win money at the 8-5 progressives, but also, the **winning strategies** for 10s or better, deuces wild, joker's wild, flat-top, progressive and special options features.

BE A WINNER IN JUST ONE DAY - In just one day, after learning our strategy, you will have the skills to **consistently win money** at video poker - with the odds. The strategies are easy to use under practical casino conditions.

FREE BONUS - PROFESSIONAL PROFIT EXPECTANCY FORMULA ($15 VALUE) - For serious players, we're including this free bonus essay which explains the professional profit expectancy principles of video poker and how to relate them to real dollars and cents in your game.

To order send just $50 by check or money order to:
Cardoza Publishing, P.O. Box 1500, Cooper Station, New York, NY 10276

THE CARDOZA CRAPS MASTER
Exclusive Offer! - Not Available Anywhere Else)
Three Big Strategies!

Here It is! **At last**, the **secrets** of the **Grande-Gold Power Sweep, Molliere's Monte Carlo Turnaround** and the **Montarde-D'Girard Double Reverse** - three big strategies - are made available and presented for the **first time anywhere!** These powerful strategies are designed for the serious craps player, one wishing to bring the best odds and strategies to hot tables, cold tables and choppy tables.

1. THE GRANDE-GOLD POWER SWEEP (HOT TABLE STRATEGY)
This **dynamic strategy** takes maximum advantage of hot tables and shows you how to amass small **fortunes quickly** when numbers are being thrown fast and furious. The Grande-Gold stresses aggressive betting on wagers the house has no edge on! This previously unreleased strategy will make you a powerhouse at a hot table.

2. MOLLIERE'S MONTE CARLO TURNAROUND (COLD TABLE STRATEGY)
For the player who likes betting against the dice, Molliere's Monte Carlo Turnaround shows how to turn a cold table into hot cash. Favored by an exclusive circle of professionals who will play nothing else, the uniqueness of this strongman strategy is that the vast majority of bets **give absolutely nothing away to the casino!**

3.MONTARDE-D'GIRARD DOUBLE REVERSE (CHOPPY TABLE STRATEGY)
This **new** strategy is the **latest development** and the **most exciting strategy** to be designed in recent years. **Learn how** to play the optimum strategies against the tables when the dice run hot and cold (a choppy table) with no apparent reason. **The Montarde-d'Girard Double Reverse** shows how you can **generate big profits** while less knowledgeable players are ground out by choppy dice. And of course, the majority of our bets give nothing away to the casino!

BONUS!!!
Order now, and you'll receive **The Craps Master-Professional Money Management Formula** ($15 value) **absolutely free!** Necessary for serious players and **used by the pros**, the **Craps Master Formula** features the unique **stop-loss ladder.**

The Above Offer is Not Available Anywhere Else. You Must Order Here.
To order send $75 $50 (plus postage and handling) by check or money order to:
Cardoza Publishing, P.O. Box 1500, Cooper Station, New York, NY 10276